The Seeds of Learning

A Cognitive Processing Model for Speech, Language, Literacy, and Executive Functioning

Tera Sumpter, M.A., CCC-SLP

Cover and book design by splane.
Cover illustration by Dan Pedersen.

ISBN 978-1-7367978-0-8

Published by
ELH Publishing, LLC

Printed in the United States of America.

All names and identifying information in client reports discussed in this book have been changed.

Contents

The world as we have created it is a process of our thinking. It cannot be changed without changing our thinking.

—Albert Einstein

The only way that we can live is if we grow. The only way that we can grow is if we change. The only way that we can change is if we learn. The only way we can learn is if we are exposed. And the only way that we can become exposed is if we throw ourselves out into the open. Do it. Throw yourself.

—C. JoyBell C.

Prologue

I have always seen the field of speech-language pathology a bit differently from the majority. During graduate school, I wasn't just reading the material being presented. I was also reading the literature and research of psychologists, neurologists, neuroscientists, occupational therapists, and linguists. I saw beyond just speech and language. I was fascinated by the concept of neuroplasticity, the brain's ability to reorganize synaptic connections due to learning and experience. I wanted to apply this concept to how therapy was done in our field.

I wanted to understand the WHY behind the deficits I was learning about in graduate school. I wanted to see the big picture of learning and how it all fit together. I asked all the questions and challenged many of the mainstream ideas, behaviors that, during graduate school, were supported by some remarkable professors and scorned by others.

Here I am 12+ years later, and I am still pushing the boundaries. I am continuing to ask all the questions and read loads of research from numerous different fields. My goal is to reshape how we assess and treat children with learning difficulties.

My integrated cognitive processing model is comprehensive, incorporating the brain functions necessary for learning–from language development to executive functioning, from visual imagery of symbols to speech development. By isolating cognitive function, it gets to the root of the challenges experienced by individuals who struggle to learn. This comprehensive approach uniquely helps explain *why* children with speech disorders struggle to read, *why* children with attention deficits struggle to learn, and *why* so many children with reading difficulties struggle with math.

Children who face learning challenges need for speech-language practitioners, educators, and other health-care professionals to keep pushing the envelope, challenging the status quo of understandings about how children learn.

Acknowledgments

This book was born from my brain only because I have been fortunate enough to have had such incredibly supportive people in my life. To my muses, Emma Tuleta and Hannah Lahiff, you inspire me, challenge me and make me so much better. I cannot wait to see what the future brings. Thank you.

To my forever friend Kelly Bryan, you are my constant, my biggest fan, and the one who gets me back up when I've been knocked down. You believe in me more than I believe in myself. I couldn't do life without you. There aren't enough "thank yous" for you. I love you beyond.

To my dear friends Brigid Kimbrell and Emily Cudnik, you two have been with me from the beginning. I am so incredibly thankful for your friendship, love, laughter, and unwavering support. You give me so much courage, and for that I am forever grateful. You both are a huge part of Seeds of Learning and this book. From the bottom of my heart, thank you.

To Dr. Myrita Wilhite and Dr. Tony Sahley, thank you for being constant supports and seeing my potential when the attacks were flying my way. You two saved my sanity through graduate school. Thank you.

To The One and Only Judy Heyer, I will never be able to fully express the appreciation and gratitude that I have for you. Your belief in me and my work has never wavered, and for that I am beyond thankful. You were my "safe place" in graduate school. You are truly one of my favorite people of all time, and I feel so incredibly honored to have you in my life as a mentor and a friend. Thank you.

To Amanda Santill, you are the reason this book exists. You! Your support, laughter, friendship, and love have meant more than you will ever know. Thank you for continuing to tell me what the plan is and forcing me back to work. You are one of the most incredible humans I have ever known. I am beyond thankful for you.

To Ed Eyhusen, thank you for being such an incredible support in the early stages of this project. You gave me the confidence to keep going when I needed it the most. You are truly the dandiest person I know. Thank you.

To Sarah Lane, your guidance, patience, support, creativity, and brilliance have made this book possible. You singlehandedly saved this book from being tossed in the fire. Thank you for saving my sanity and my life's work and helping me present it to the world. I appreciate you.

To all of my Seeds of Learning families who have printed hands on my tree and love on my heart over the years, thank you for sharing your children and your families with me. You and your children have been the most profound teachers I have ever had. This book would not exist without each one of your children. Thank you for your trust, support, and love over the years.

To my mom, thank you for always believing in me. You always made me feel like anything was possible and that I could accomplish anything I set my mind to. Thank you for paving the way for me to be an independent fierce female and never squashing my fire. I love you.

To my dad, thank you for teaching me the value of hard work, forcing me to prove myself, and then opening all of the doors you possibly could for me. We stand on the shoulders of giants. Dad, you are those shoulders for me. Thank you. I love you.

To my husband, Kjell, you have made all of my dreams come true. Thank you for being my continuous support system and #1 pep-talk giver. You are my rock and the source of all great things in my life. Thank you for loving my dreams as much as I do, creating space for me to pursue them, and sacrificing so that I can dream big. I am forever grateful that I get to do life with you. I love you.

To my children, Emma, Lily, and Hannah, you may not remember or realize it now, but there were so many years when you had to be quiet in the basement while I spent uninterrupted time with other children. You used to come into my therapy office and say, "Mommy, I want to be one of your clients." Baby girls, you will always be the most special children in the world to me. You are truly the most magical people I have ever known. I am beyond honored and grateful to be your mom. Thank you for always being so loving and kind to all of the children who came through our door for so many years. Thank you for sharing me with other kids so that I could help them. I know that has not always been easy. But always remember, you are my number-one loves.

Introduction

Today in our society, we are label happy. We are quick to slap labels on anyone and anything. Our children are labeled as having dyslexia, specific language disability, intellectual disability, speech and language impairment, developmental language disorder, dysgraphia, learning disability, processing disorder, ADD/ADHD, autism, and more. I understand that these labels help us classify students, but for what purpose? What information do these diagnoses offer us? What information do these labels provide us clinically? Yes, they can point us in the right direction, but they can also point us in the wrong direction. Do they tell us where the breakdowns are for a particular student? Do they show us how a child is processing information? Do they help us write treatment plans? Do they help us devise specific enough goals? I would argue that they simply do not.

What we've been missing for far too long is that many of these labels have overlapping cognitive components. When we label a child with dyslexia and language impairment, for example, we're missing the fact that there might actually be a shared underlying cognitive deficit. Or how about when we label a child with ADHD and language disorder? What are the underlying cognitive deficits driving these impairments we're seeing? There is always a connection.

The beauty of using an integrated cognitive approach to assessment and intervention is that we collect knowledge about how a student is actually processing information. Such an approach allows us to find the cognitive breakdowns so that we can write goals that will strengthen processing rather than simply putting a bandage on surface-level symptoms.

Oftentimes, the therapy we provide students is in the form of strategies. These methods can frequently act as crutches. Rather than using an approach focused on strategies, we should focus on strengthening cognitive deficits. Research in neuroplasticity shows us that we can restructure how the brain processes information. So let's start there.

Reuven Feuerstein, a clinical, developmental, and cognitive psychologist, wrote this about structural changes: "Structural changes refer not to isolated events but to the organism's manner of interacting with, i.e., acting on and responding to, sources of information. Thus, a *structural change*, once set in motion, will determine the future course of an individual's development" (Feuerstein, 2006).

Our goal as practitioners should be to stimulate a student's brain to strengthen areas of cognitive weakness. If we can accomplish that, we move our students toward independence, and independence should always be our number-one goal.

So much of education and intervention today is driven by one thing: data. Data leads to a diagnosis and that is where most of us stop. Children are not data. Children are not a diagnosis. Children are not something that can be categorized based on standard scores and percentiles. Like all of us, children are complex beings with vast cognitive, social-emotional, fine motor, gross motor, and sensory system processing that must function together for success. We must look beyond the standard scores and labels to find the patterns of difficulty. We must dive into the warning signs of struggle to see where the breakdown is occurring. We must stop taking our wondrous children who come to us as curious, diverse learners and try to cram them into a one-size-fits-all model. We must stop focusing on arbitrary test scores to tell us if our children are okay. We must stop trying to create one kind of learner. We must meet our children where they are in development, guide them along the learning process, and support them exactly where they need supporting.

We need to stop trying to fit everyone into the same mold. The geniuses in our society think outside the box. They see the world in ways that others cannot begin to comprehend. These people are not "standardized." These individuals started out as children who viewed the world and their learning in just that way–differently. If we continue to classify our children by standardized means and educate them in that manner, we will lose our geniuses. Enough is enough. It is time to do better.

This book is intended to be a guide based on my years of research analysis and synthesis and clinical experience. This book was written for anyone who wants to view childhood learning struggles in a different manner. I hope you find it helpful.
You can find me on Instagram at @terasumpter_slp, where I frequently share education and therapy ideas, or reach me via email at tera@seedsoflearningllc.com.

1
The Big Picture: An Integrated Model of Cognitive Processing

Let's begin by considering the difference between function and skill. Our brain has certain *functions* that it develops. Think of the function as a muscle that allows us to complete certain tasks. For example, if our bicep muscles are strong enough, we can perform the task of lifting heavy objects with our arms. Cognition works in a similar fashion. We have certain functions that, if strong enough, will allow us to perform certain tasks or acquire certain skills. This concept is important as we need to be addressing the underlying cognitive functions or processes, rather than plugging away to address every little skill with which our students need help. If we help a student strengthen cognitive "muscles," they should be able to acquire cognitive skills more independently. Obviously, every student's potential level of independence will vary, but cognitive function should always be the primary goal.

Figure 1.1 is my model of integrated cognitive processing. This model allows us to get to the core of a student's learning difficulty. It also allows us to look past diagnoses and labels to reveal the root of the struggle. It can help us see where the breakdown in processing is occurring. Additionally, it shows us what development is impacting other development. Finally, this model provides us with a clear framework for assessment and treatment.

This cognitive processing model offers an integrated and comprehensive approach to assessment and treatment. A variety of cognitive processes are involved in learning, including speech development, phonological processing, visual imagery processing for symbols, visual imagery processing for concepts, receptive and expressive language, and executive functions. Weakness in one or all of these areas can greatly affect a student's ability to learn and succeed academically. It is imperative that professionals use a comprehensive and integrative cognitive model to assess and treat students so that a complete picture is obtained.

Cognitive processes do not function in isolation. They are all connected. Because they are integrated, they function together and therefore should be evaluated and treated comprehensively.

Figure 1.1 Integrated Cognitive Processing

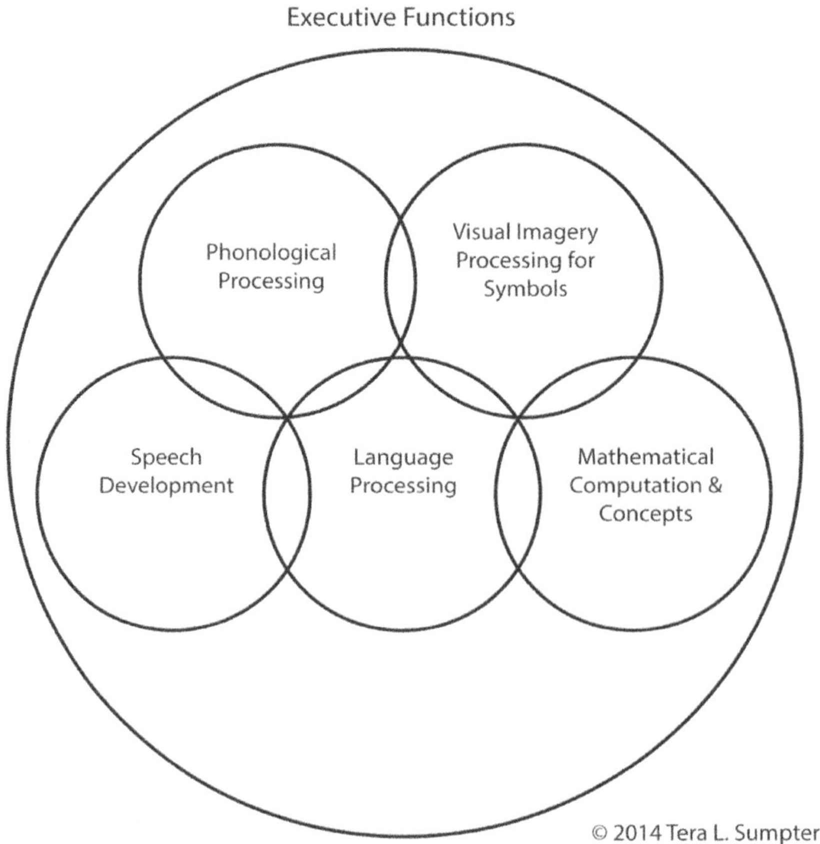

2
Subsystems of the Model

We will now look at each system contained with the model in greater detail.

Speech Processing

Figure 2.1 Speech Development as Part of Executive Functions

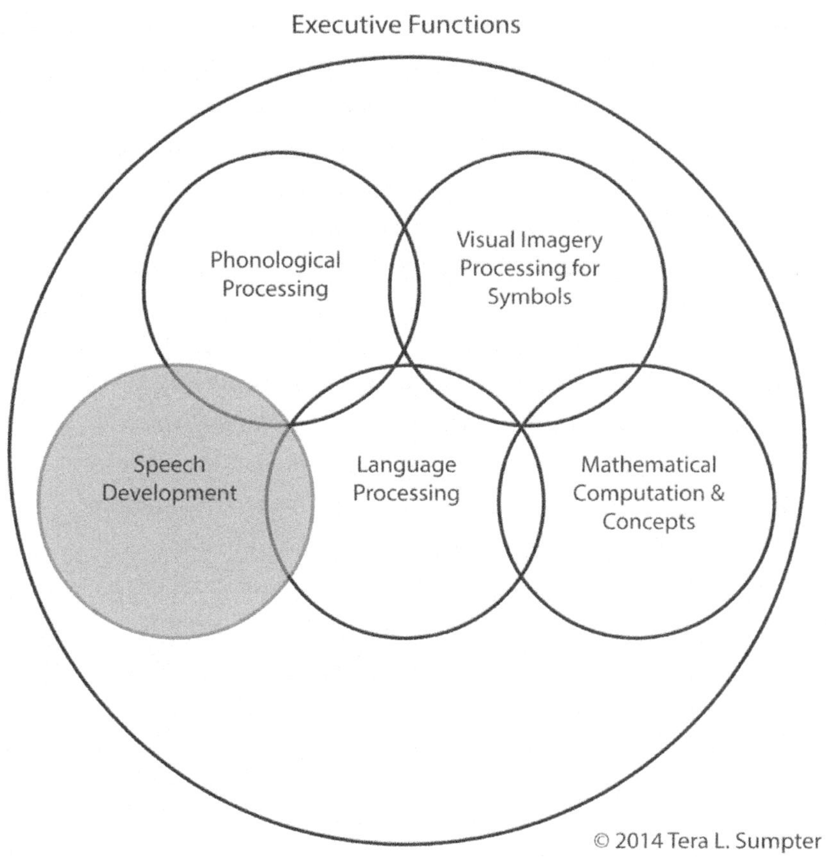

Let's begin with our first cognitive subsystem, speech processing. What is speech? Speech is simply the sounds we use to communicate. It is how we verbalize individual phonemes and words. Speech processing is not about meaning. It is simply the sounds we produce.

Speech processing involves five body systems: respiratory, phonatory, resonatory, articulatory, and neurological. All five of these systems have to be properly developed, integrated, and coordinated for the purpose of speech processing.

When a baby begins developing speech in the form of cooing and babbling, a connection starts to form in the brain between what the baby feels in the mouth and what she hears. For example, mom says, "bottle" and baby attempts to repeat mom by saying /ba/. Baby's cognition takes note of what her speech processing system just performed, as well as what she heard. As her speech processing system matures, she is able to repeat after mom more accurately, all the while refining what is recorded in her phonological processing system (the part of the brain that processes sound).

Let's recall what we discussed in Chapter 1 about functions versus skills. Speech processing is a cognitive function. When appropriate speech development takes place, we see the acquisition of certain skills. When speech processing develops appropriately, we tend to see the acquisition of skills such as cooing, babbling, verbal sound play, and articulation.

Without proper speech development, we see delays in most of these skills. Additionally, the phonological processing system is unable to improve and strengthen to an appropriate level due to the lack of speech input. As a result, children with speech development issues tend to have deficits in the development of their phonological processing. Furthermore, the majority of children with speech sound disorders experience difficulty with reading, as phonological processing is a key component of literacy development. **When addressing speech development, a**

therapist must also address phonological processing.

Speech processing issues to be aware of include articulation disorders, dysarthria, childhood apraxia of speech, phonological disorders, voicing, and fluency disorders.

Phonological Processing

The next subsystem of the cognitive model is phonological processing, the system of the brain that processes sound. We could say that it is the "hearing" part of the brain. (This should not be confused with the speech disorder term *phonological processes.)* Our phonological system is responsible for processing tiny units of sound known as *phonemes* (for example, /b/, /a/, /th/, /i/). These are sounds in isolation. Phonemes are the building blocks of our speech productions and language. This area of processing develops very early on beginning in the womb (Moon et al., 2013). We often don't think much about phonemes until we learn phonics, learning that "b" says /b/ or "o" says /o/.

Our phonological systems are also responsible for processing connected units of sound called *syllables.* When we put phonemes together, we create syllable structures. Syllable structures can be as simple as CV/VC (consonant-vowel/vowel-consonant), like "go" or "up," and as complex as 7+ syllables, like "conceptualization." Here is a breakdown of the phonological hierarchy (see Appendix A for example words of these syllable structures):

CV/VC
CVC
CCV/VCC
CCVC/CVCC
CCVCC
CCCVCC
2 syllable

3 syllable
4 syllable
5 syllable
6 syllable
7+ syllable

It should be noted that when moving up the phoneme hierarchy from three to four sounds, two processing aspects are added, not just one: an extra sound plus a blend. Children with speech deficits may find this step from three to four sounds extra difficult as a result. At times, a half step in the forms of CCV and VCC syllable structures may be necessary. For example, CVC is three sounds. CCV/VCC is three sounds with a blend. If we jump from CVC to CCVC/CVCC, we're jumping from three sounds to four sounds PLUS a blend.

Within this hierarchy of sound structures, children must be able to identify the sounds they are processing and the order in which they are processing them. For example, given the stimulus /blimp/, we would want a child to be able to tell us that /blimp/ has five sounds, which are /b/-/l/-/i/-/m/-/p/. We also want children to be able to manipulate sounds in words. For example, take the word "cat" and change the /c/ to /h/. What is the word now? "Hat." That manipulation of sounds within a syllable structure is an important developmental component of the phonological system.

Understanding where in this hierarchy of sound structures our students are struggling is key to intervention. As we saw in the previous section on speech processing, phonological and speech processing are closely connected. Research shows us that children with childhood apraxia of speech are at risk for phonemic awareness and reading delays (McNeill et al., 2009). In fact, one study showed that phonemic awareness intervention improved speech impairments (Dodd & Gillon, 2009). With that said, we know our children with speech impairments are going to be at risk for phonological processing weaknesses. As we will see later on, phonological processing is a key component of literacy development. Therefore, we can begin to connect the dots that our students with speech deficits may develop poor phonological processing skills and thus struggle when it comes to reading.

Figure 2.2 Phonological Processing as Part of Executive Functions

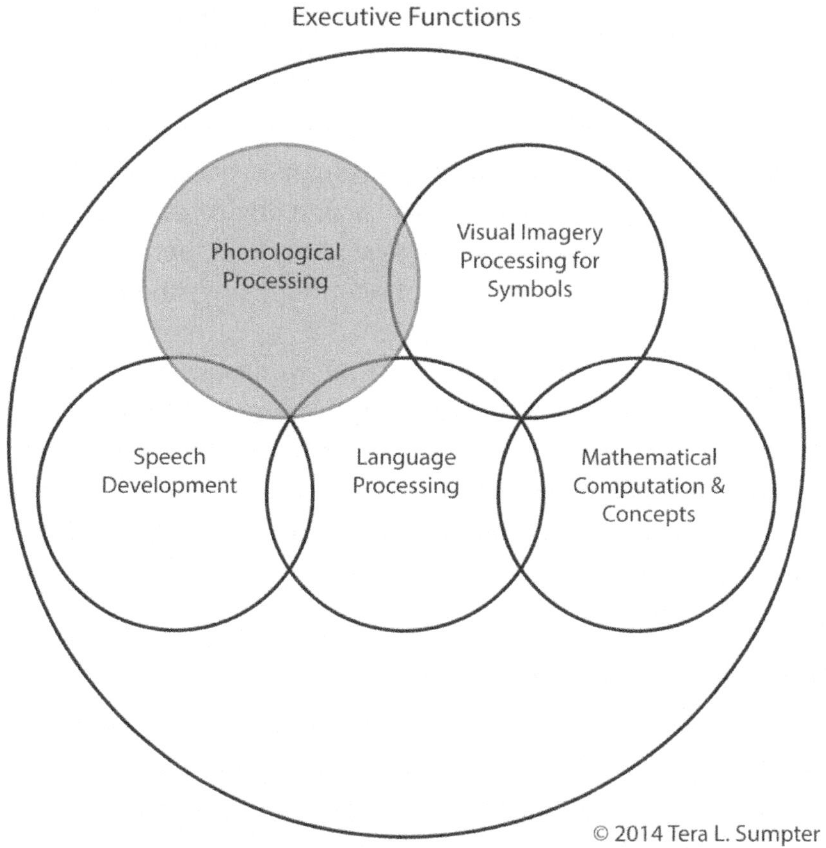

A 28-year follow-up study of adults with a history of moderate phonological disorder revealed that, in comparison to control subjects, they had received lower grades in high school, required more remedial academic services throughout their school careers, and completed fewer years of formal education (Felsenfield et al., 1994). It is clear that speech sound and phonological processing disorders significantly impact all later academic learning, which is important clinical information. When we see our speech disorder students beginning to struggle academically, we know that, because cognitive processing is all connected, the problem must be addressed in an integrated fashion. **Speech therapy should never be done in isolation. It should always be done in conjunction with phonological therapy.**

Let's return to the idea of cognitive function versus skills: When a student has an appropriately developed phonological processing system, we tend to see an accompanying development of skills such as imitation, phonological awareness, phonics acquisition, decoding for reading, phonetic spelling, and reading accuracy.

It is important to note that, any time we suspect a student is struggling to process sound, we must refer them to an audiologist for an audiological examination to rule out a hearing impairment. Only then, once a hearing impairment is ruled out, can we move forward with deeper examination of the phonological processing system.

Client Report: Molly

Molly, a 7-year-old female, was struggling with literacy development. She had a history of a speech delay for which she received speech therapy for three years. When reading, Molly rarely sounded out words, often guessing based off of the first letter. Her spelling was rarely phonetic, and her reading comprehension was poor. After psychological testing, Molly was given the diagnosis of dyslexia. She had been receiving reading intervention at school with minimal progress. Upon a comprehensive cognitive evaluation, Molly was found to have a reading impairment characterized by weakness in her phonological processing region of cognition at the 2-sound level (CV/VC). Her reading intervention, though phonologically based, had been ineffective because the intervention assumed stability at the CVC level, and Molly's deficits began at just 2 sounds.

Language Processing

What is language processing? In its simplest form, language is giving meaning to sound. Language occurs when we attach a concept or mental representation to a unit of sounds. For example, when a baby understands that the CVC unit of sounds /dog/ represents the furry little white animal that barks in his house, he has developed language.

Steven Pinker, a cognitive psychologist and linguist at Harvard University, said in an interview, "I don't think that we think in language, or think in words. I think we think in visual images, we think in auditory images, we think in abstract propositions about what is true about what" (Pinker, 2008). Albert Einstein said, "If I can't picture it, I can't understand it" (Horgan, 1991). **Mental pictures are what anchor language in our brain.**

Take a second to think about your favorite vacation. What happened in your mind? Ideally, you saw images of where you went and what you did, like a white sandy beach with crystal clear water and palm trees. **The ability to visualize language is the key to language development, comprehension, and**

organized expression. I refer to this visual imagery as a three-dimensional type of imagery, as opposed to the two-dimensional visual imagery for symbols that we will address in the next section.

Figure 2.3 Language Processing as Part of Executive Functions

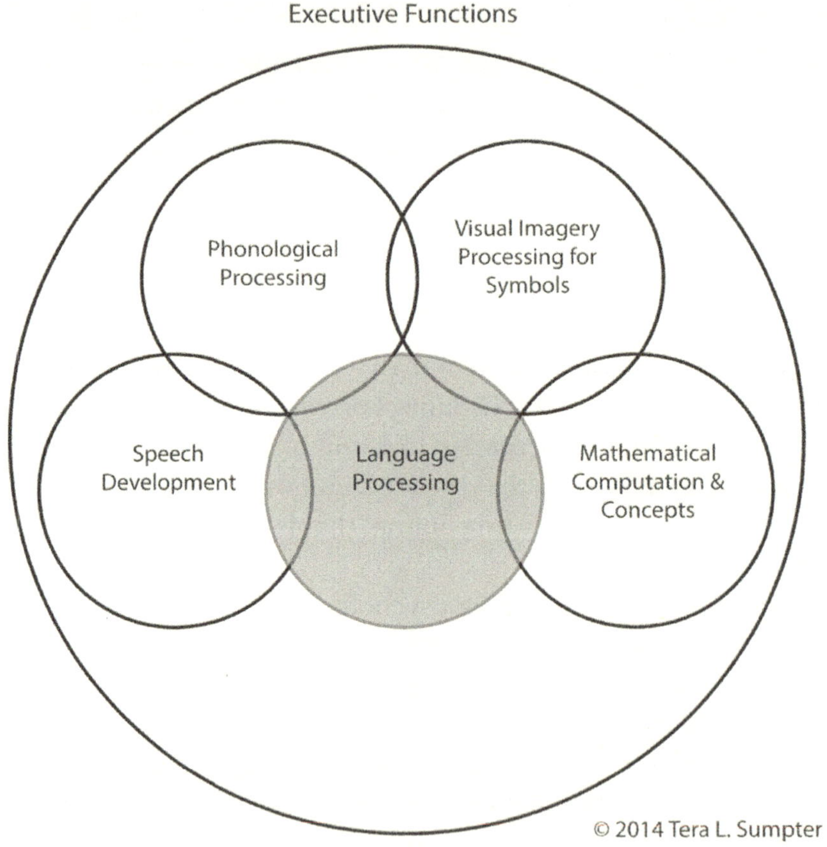

The ability to visualize or create mental representations in our mind is what allows us to think, develop language, and self-regulate (executive functioning). We see this development occur early in life when a baby acquires object permanence. This develops around 8 to 12 months of age. Mom leaves the room, and

baby no longer cries. Why does this happen? I
that mom still exists. How does she know this
a mental image of mom in her mind. Before
typically cries when mom leaves the room b
is gone forever. The development of a ment
baby to be comforted by the fact that mom still exists.

Around 12 to 18 months, toddlers develop more sophisticated mental representations. An object can be hidden in their visual field, and they can retrieve it. How did they know where it was? They held an image of the object in their mind long enough to be able to find it.

By 18 to 24 months of age, a child's object permanence becomes fully developed. The child is able to generate a mental image, hold it in her mind, and manipulate it to solve problems. It is around this same developmental period when children begin pretend play. The child picks up a banana and says, "Hello?" pretending it is a telephone. This development occurs because the child has created a mental representation of a phone in his mind while utilizing a different object as a representation.

As children continue to develop, this visualization system becomes more sophisticated, allowing them cognitively to generate, store, manipulate, and retrieve all kinds of information in all different dimensions of time (past, present, future).

How is this mental workspace of images developed? It can be developed through any activity that stimulates the imagination to create pictures such as pretend play, reading to children, creating art, and reading to one's self. However, our students are spending longer amounts of time on technological devices that *provide* images to their brains. We need to return to activities in which their brains are forced to *generate* images. The brain's ability to generate, retain, and recall visual pictures is what will ultimately stimulate language development.

ology and Pragmatics

Language is a complex cognitive subsystem that involves many components, including semantics, syntax, and morphology. In a traditional view of language, phonology and pragmatics would also be included as components of language. However, I would suggest that phonology is a cognitive processing region that functions on its own to acquire its own skills and is accessed and integrated for the purpose of language. This separation of functioning between language and phonology is evidenced when we ask children to read nonsense words. There is no language involved in these words, yet children who have strong phonological processing can still read them. As a result, we see that phonological processing can function separately from language.

As for pragmatics, it is a function of executive functioning, which will be discussed in Chapter 3. With that being said, as evidenced in the model, phonology and language processing certainly overlap and intertwine for the purpose of cognitive development; and pragmatics is the functional outcome of self-regulation.

Receptive and Expressive Pathways

Language processing includes receptive and expressive pathways. These two cognitive functions are not the same in the brain and, therefore, both have to be addressed separately. For example, just because a student can point to the pen when asked to do so does not mean that he can say, "pen" when asked to label it. Although the stimulus of the pen is the same, the routes in and out of the brain for identification and labeling are different.

If the connection between mental representation and sound develops sufficiently, a student develops the skills of language processing. These include **receptive language skills** of auditory comprehension, such as understanding oral language, following directions, acquiring vocabulary, understanding concrete and abstract concepts, understanding relationships between words and ideas, and comprehending the world around them.

Expressive language skills include expressing wants and needs verbally, with an Augmentative and Alternative Communication (AAC) method or in writing; answering questions accurately and appropriately; interacting with the world; and using appropriate vocabulary, semantics, grammar, and thought organization when communicating.

Visual Imagery Processing for Symbols

Visual imagery processing of symbols is a cognitive process that allows us to recognize, retain, and recall various types of symbols. It is an integral part of cognitive processing for reading, writing, and math.

Think of the related area of the brain as the part that "sees" symbols. Examples of symbols include letters, numbers, math signs (e.g., +, ×, ≥, =), and punctuation marks (e.g., ?, !, ., ;). Unlike the 3-dimensional visual imagery used to store language, only 2-dimensional imagery is required for symbols, which cannot be rotated or flipped. These images must be stored in a static, unchanging manner. Our brain has literally to lock down these symbols the way they were seen.

This concept can be difficult for some children when print is introduced. If I hold up my cell phone and ask what it is, it is a cell phone. If I flip it around, it is still a cell phone. If I rotate it facedown, it is still a cell phone. We cannot do that with symbols. If I hold up a letter "b," it is a "b." If I flip it, it becomes a "d." If I rotate it facedown, it becomes a "p" or "q." Children have to learn that visual imagery for language can be changed in the way of perspective, but visual imagery for symbols cannot.

This area of cognition is located in a region of the brain referred to as the *visual word form area* (VWFA) (Cohen et al., 2002). When we are born, this area recognizes faces. As we are exposed to letters, numbers, and print, this region of the brain begins to reorganize. One of the lead neuroscientists in this field, Dr. Stanislas Dehaene, has written a phenomenal book on the topic, *Reading in the Brain*. According to Dehaene, this cognitive area, when developed, is responsible for sight word acquisition, orthographic spelling, fluent contextual reading, reading rate, math fact acquisition, and math computation skills.

For children with weakness in visual imagery processing for symbols, the introduction of cursive writing can be problematic. Cursive is a completely new symbol set. In addition, some computer type fonts can be troublesome for children who struggle with this two-dimensional imagery, as again they are different symbol sets.

Client Report: Sam

Sam, a 10-year-old male, was struggling with literacy development. When reading, Sam tended to sound out most words, even words he had just seen. His reading could be described as choppy and dysfluent. Sam's spelling was often phonetic. He displayed frequent letter and number reversals. His reading comprehension was poor. Sam also made careless mistakes on math work, such as by subtracting when the indicated symbol was +.

A psychologist had diagnosed Sam with dyslexia. He had been receiving phonologically based reading intervention for several years with little improvement.

After a comprehensive evaluation, Sam was found to have a reading impairment characterized by weakness in his visual imagery processing for symbols. This weakness impaired Sam's ability to acquire sight words, spell orthographically, read fluently contextually, and process math symbols adequately.

Figure 2.4 Visual Imagery Processing for Symbols as Part of Executive Functions

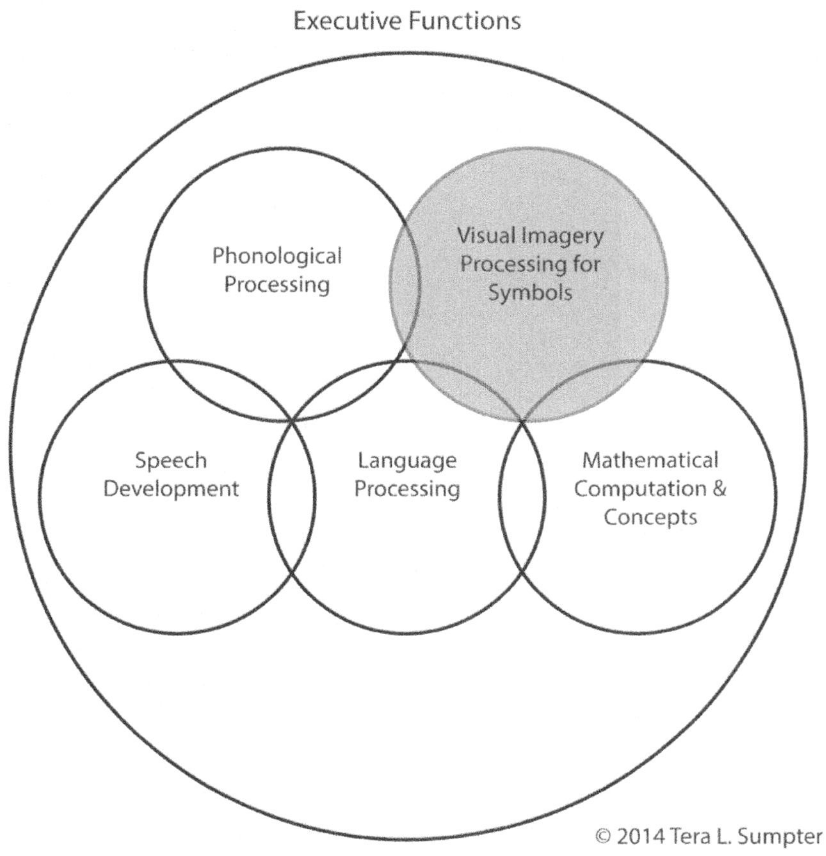

Math Computation and Concepts

Math = Language + Visual Imagery for Symbols + Executive Functioning

Math is a cognitive combination of language and visual imagery for symbols processing. Math introduces new vocabulary and concepts (language) as well as new symbol sets (numbers and math signs). When a child is struggling in math, determining the underlying deficit area is key to intervention, as, for example, the deficit could also be in executive functioning. The EF demands for math are enormous. We'll consider more on that in Chapter 3.

Figure 2.5 Math Computation and Concepts as Part of Executive Functions

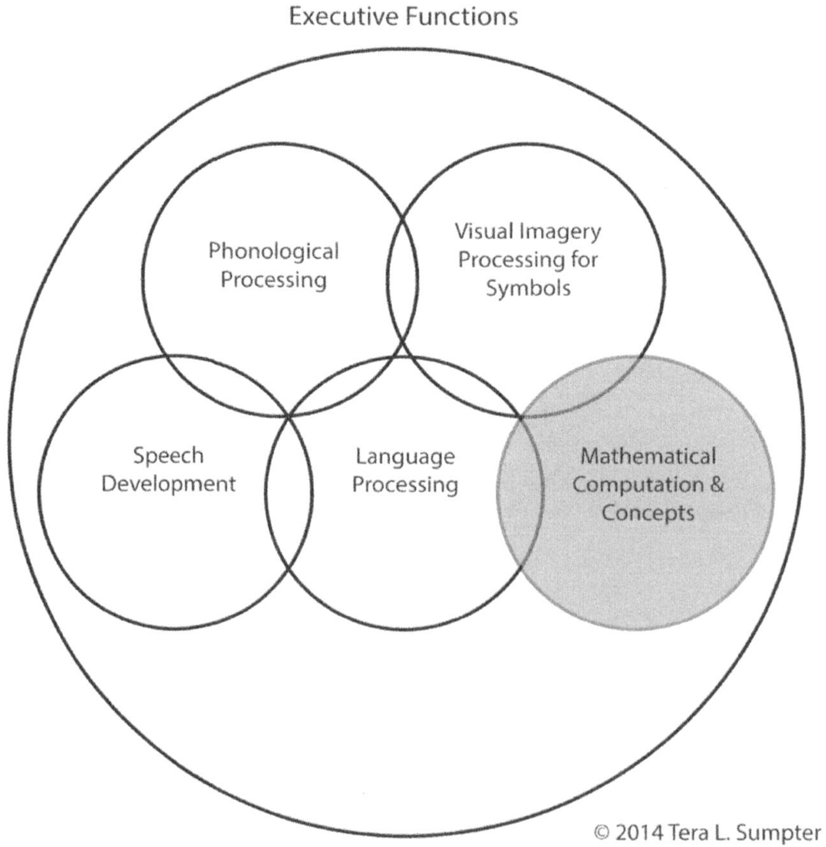

3
Executive Functions: The Self-Regulatory System

The executive functioning system is our overarching, all-encompassing regulatory system of cognition. This system is the "boss" of the brain. It makes sure that all of the subsystems of cognition are doing what they are supposed to be doing. It also acts like an orchestra conductor, coordinating and integrating all of the various parts of cognition to create a seamless, harmonious input and output (see Figure 3.1).

In this book, I will define *executive functioning* using Dr. George McCloskey's skill cluster model. I have chosen McCloskey's skill clusters as my model for executive functioning assessment and treatment because I have found this model to be the most detailed and comprehensive. This thorough approach to defining executive functioning allows me as a practitioner to be very specific about a client's deficit areas and levels of breakdown. The more precise I can be in the identification of deficit areas, the more targeted and effective my therapy can be.

For the purpose of this book, I am simplifying Dr. McCloskey's model. For a more in-depth examination of the executive functioning system, I highly recommend his book, *Assessment and Intervention for Executive Function Difficulties.*

The executive function system can be broken down into skill clusters as shown in the organization proposed by George McCloskey and colleagues in 2009 (see Figure 3.2).

A hallmark of executive function deficit is inconsistency in performance. One moment a child might be "connected" and receiving the presented information, while the next moment he might be zoned out and missing it. One day he may do well on a test and the next day do very poorly.

Figure 3.1 Executive Functions

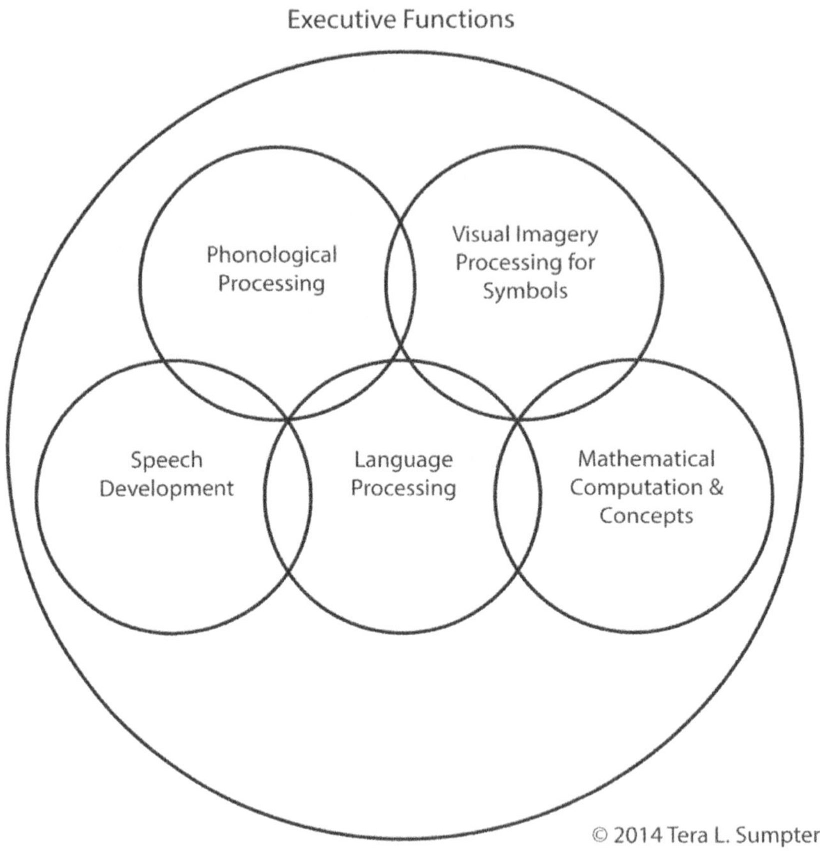

The impact of executive function weakness on learning is immense. Children develop speech and language by paying attention to the adults around them throughout development. When children are not "connected" or listening to their adult models during development, they miss large amounts of information. We may see gaps in any or all aspects of cognitive development, gaps in knowledge, difficulty acquiring and retaining information, and difficulty generating new ideas and initiating tasks. These affected children may be unorganized, forgetful, inflexible, easily distracted, and often off-task. They may rush through assignments with poor self-monitoring and self-correction, or they may seem to take forever due to poor focus, pace, time sense, prioritization, and initiation. When tasks have multiple steps and require layers of planning to execute, children with executive function difficulties may easily become overwhelmed.

Figure 3.2 Skill Clusters

ATTENTION
Perception
Focus
Sustained Attention

ENGAGEMENT
Energize
Initiate
Inhibit
Stop
Pause
Flexible
Shift

OPTIMIZATION
Self-Monitor
Self-Modulate
Balance
Self-Correct

EFFICIENCY
Sense Time
Pace
Sequence
Execute

MEMORY
Hold
Manipulate
Store
Retrieve

INQUIRY
Anticipate
Gauge
Analyze
Estimate Time
Compare

SOLUTION
Generate
Associate
Prioritize
Plan
Organize
Decide

(McCloskey et al., 2009)

These children are far too often referred to as "lazy" or as "not working hard enough," or they may be seen as behavior problems. They may have difficulty self-modulating their emotions and display outbursts or tantrums or react in ways that do not match the triggering factor.

Pragmatics (social) development is a function of our executive functioning system, and children with executive function difficulty often struggle socially. Social interaction or pragmatic development requires focus and sustained attention to a conversational partner. You have to hear and process what the other person is saying in order to respond appropriately. Social interaction also requires inhibition. A child must inhibit her own desire to blurt out and interrupt, grab a toy away from a friend, or shove a peer in frustration in order to make friends and be socially appropriate. Inhibition is also necessary for turn taking during a conversation or social interaction.

From a diagnostic standpoint, these children can often be difficult to diagnose because they may present with other comorbidities like language delay/disorder, speech delay/disorder, learning disability, dyslexia or other reading impairment, specific learning impairment, pragmatic disorder, and so on. As professionals, we must determine if the executive function impairment is the deficit driving all of the other learning impairments with which the child is presenting.

In many cases, the executive function impairment indeed causes the other learning disabilities simply because the child is not focused or connected to the world around him or her. This is particularly true when it comes to language development. Most children acquire language simply by being immersed in a language-rich environment. When children do not perceive their environment (like children with autism spectrum disorder) or do not consistently attend to their environment (like children with ADD/ADHD), they will undoubtedly display delays and disorders in speech and language development. Before learning can take place, a child must first perceive his environment and then attend to his environment. If these two executive functioning skills—perception and attention—are not adequately developed, then learning is typically impaired.

To put it bluntly, **sometimes the information gets in, and sometimes it doesn't** (see Figure 3.3).

Figure 3.3 Occasional Information Barriers Through Inadequately Developed Executive Functioning

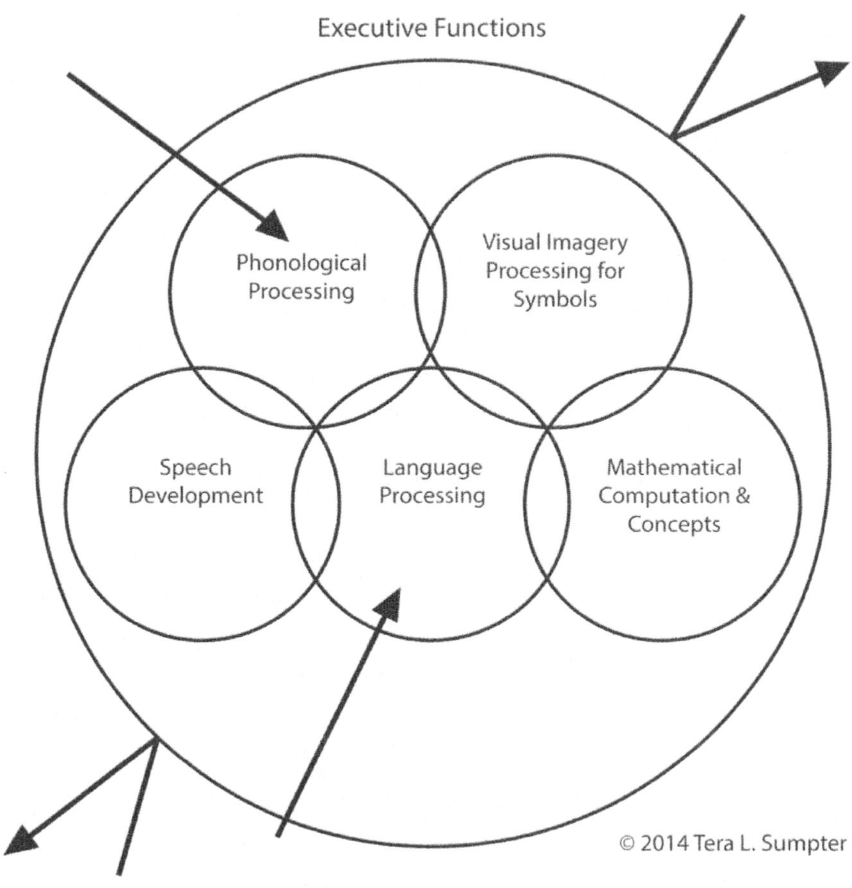

We are always required to use executive functions. There is no activity, no task, no activity in which we do not have to use our executive functioning skills. This point is critical when we talk about assessment. Every test, whether it involves speech, language, reading, psychology, social studies, or math, is also testing a child's executive functioning skills. Why is this important? Because oftentimes a child will present with deficits in other cognitive areas *as a result* of an executive functioning impairment. So in reality, the perceived deficit is not the root cause but actually a symptom. We must always be looking for the root cause of the impairments we are seeing.

Client Report: Tom

Tom, a 6-year-old male in first grade, was struggling with all aspects of speech and language development and was not successfully learning in the classroom. Tom's attention/focus had been an issue since it was first noticed around age 2. He had been diagnosed with ADHD by his pediatrician. Tom had received speech therapy for three years, two days a week for 30-minute sessions. Mom felt like there was little to no progress being made in therapy.

Tom came to see me for a comprehensive evaluation. I was unable to complete an age-appropriate evaluation due to Tom's lack of perception, focus, and sustained attention. He was able to sustain attention for approximately 30 seconds at a time. He was unable to follow 1-step commands. His expressive language was characterized by 3- to 4-word phrases with inappropriate semantics, syntax, and morphology. Word finding appeared to be very difficult for him. He was unable to participate in conversation. Tom's speech was characterized by inconsistent error patterns of consonant deletion, distortion, and substitution; blend reductions; syllable deletions; and vowel distortions. Tom was not developing literacy skills.

I diagnosed Tom with a primary diagnosis of severe executive functioning impairment characterized by deficits in perception, focus, and sustained attention; a secondary diagnosis of language disorder; and a tertiary diagnosis of speech disorder. Tom's speech and language disorders were clearly a result of his severe executive functioning impairment.

Even though this book will not address therapy, it should be noted that the first month of Tom's therapy addressed increasing his perception, focus, and sustained attention. Once we reached a 5-minute period of sustained attention after about a month of therapy, we were able to begin addressing language with an integrated language/executive functioning approach. This process will be outlined in an upcoming book. Stay tuned!

4
Application of the Model in School Settings

We can use this comprehensive integrated model to examine the cognitive processing demands required for various school subjects including reading/language arts, math, science, social studies, and a foreign language.

Literacy

Literacy development is extremely complex. It involves numerous areas of cognitive processing, namely speech, phonological, visual imagery for symbols, language, and executive functioning.

Quiet contextual reading occurs when phonological processing, visual imagery for symbols processing, and language processing integrate with regulation by the executive functioning system as seen in Figure 4.1.

Reading out loud is slightly more complex, with the addition of the speech processing center as seen in Figure 4.2. It should be noted that children with speech processing issues, namely childhood apraxia of speech, often do poorly on literacy assessments when they have to read aloud, due to poor oral motor coordination and execution, particularly when a time component is added to the assessment (e.g., read as many words as possible in 1 minute). When the oral motor system is stressed, we often see impaired performance by these children. In other words, their poor literacy scores could be a result of their impaired oral motor coordination skills rather than of literacy processing.

With that being said, the connection between speech sound disorders and literacy impairments has been well documented.

Figure 4.1 Integration of Executive Functioning System

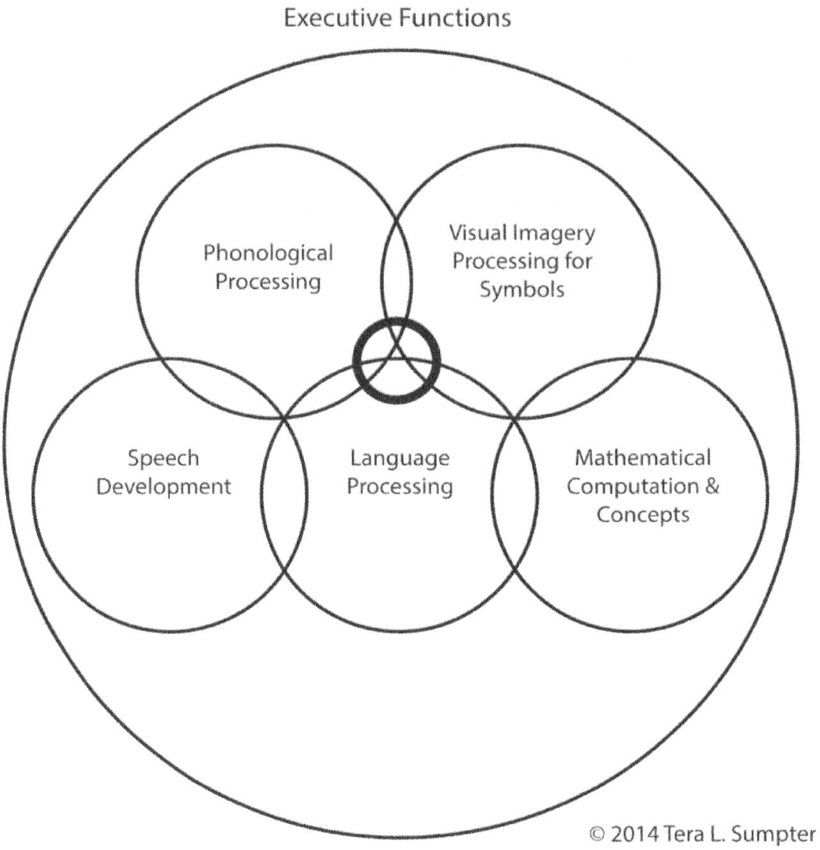

Executive Functions

Phonological Processing

Visual Imagery Processing for Symbols

Speech Development

Language Processing

Mathematical Computation & Concepts

© 2014 Tera L. Sumpter

Why is this? As previously discussed, speech development and phonological processing are intimately connected in the brain during development. These two cognitive domains cannot be separated. When speech develops inadequately, phonological processing often does too. We must address both in therapy!

So what if there is a breakdown in literacy development? **It is not enough simply to diagnose a child with dyslexia**, which by definition is simply a reading impairment. Professionals

Figure 4.2 Speech Processing Center

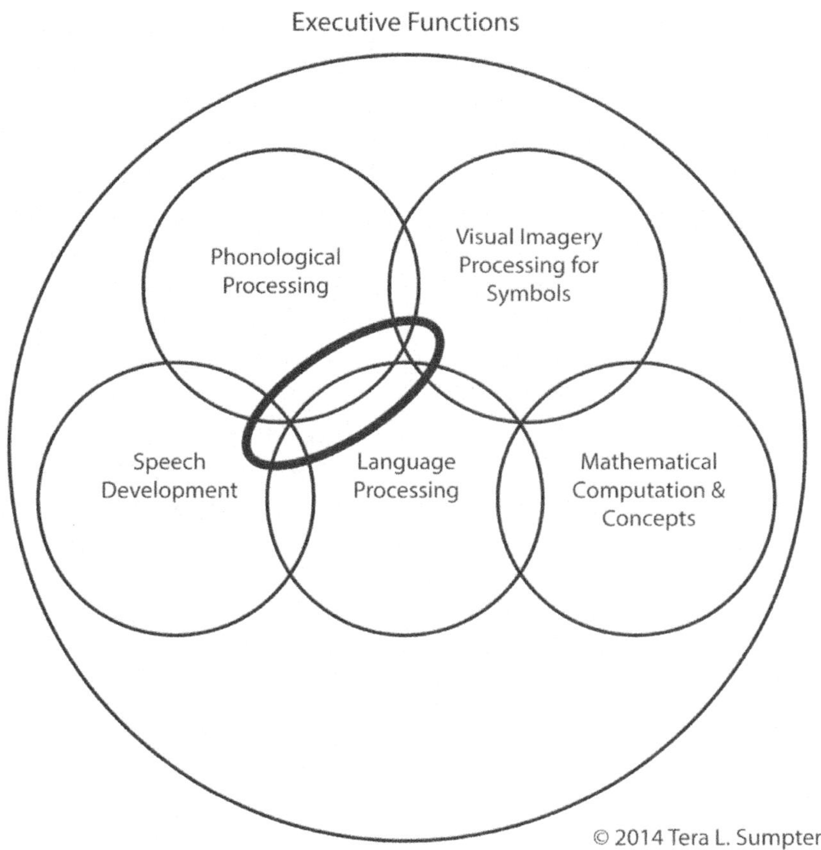

must determine (1) where in the cognitive system (subsystem or self-regulatory system) the deficit is occurring and (2) at what processing level the breakdown begins. For example, the cognitive system deficit might be occurring in the phonological processing area at the CVC level. Or the cognitive system deficit could be occurring in the visual imagery for symbols processing area at the 4-letter level. Or maybe the cognitive system deficit is in the language region at the comprehension level of 4 words. The cognitive system deficit could otherwise be in the executive functioning domain at the level of self-monitoring and self-correction.

Table 4.1 summarizes the skills developed in each cognitive domain.

Table 4.1 Cognitive Domains and Associated Literacy Skills

COGNITIVE DOMAIN	Phonological Processing	Visual Imagery Processing for Symbols (VWFA)	Language Processing	Executive Functioning
SKILLS	Phonics	Letter development	Vocabulary knowledge	Focus on text
	Decoding/sounding out	Sight word acquisition	Use of context clues to figure out unknown words	Sustained attention throughout a book or story
	Reading accuracy	Appropriate reading rate	Use of pictures to figure out text	Self-monitoring of literacy skills
	Phonetic spelling	Reading fluency	Reading comprehension	Self-correction of errors
		Orthographic spelling	Determining main idea and making inferences, predictions, associations, etc.	Planning involved in reading process (e.g., left to right reading direction, page turning)
				Integration of phonological, visual imagery for symbols, and language processing for contextual reading
				Using working memory in phonological and visual processing for sounds, letters, and language

Reading Mechanics

The two cognitive areas of phonological processing and visual imagery for symbols processing comprise what I refer to as the *mechanics* of reading. When children are learning how to read, they typically develop phonological processing skills first. We see that when they start sounding out small words. Over time, there is a shift that takes place as demonstrated in Figure 4.3. Words that have previously been decoded over and over again become stored visually by the visual imagery for symbols processing area, and the child no longer has to sound out the word. She simply recognizes the word as a sight word.

This shift from phonological to visual processing occurs at different times in development for each child. On average, it occurs around 6 to 7 years old (Dehaene, 2009). But sometimes we won't see this shift occur because the visual imagery processing domain never fully strengthens. In that case, therapy is needed to increase the processing ability of that area.

If a child has developed strong processing in the two cognitive domains necessary for reading mechanics (phonological processing and visual imagery for symbols processing), he will be able to read words on a page. However, mastering that skill does not ensure comprehension of text. Reading comprehension requires the development and integration of the language processing system, and, as discussed in Chapter 2, language processing requires visualization. Children must be able to visualize (i.e., make mental pictures of) what they read in order to comprehend it.

One of the biggest mistakes I see occur in the classroom with early readers is that they are encouraged to look at the pictures in order to "read" the book. Asking a child to use pictures to read does not strengthen her reading mechanics (phonological processing and visual imagery for symbols processing). Rather, it provides her with a language tool. If you want to strengthen

Figure 4.3 Processing Shift in Literacy Development

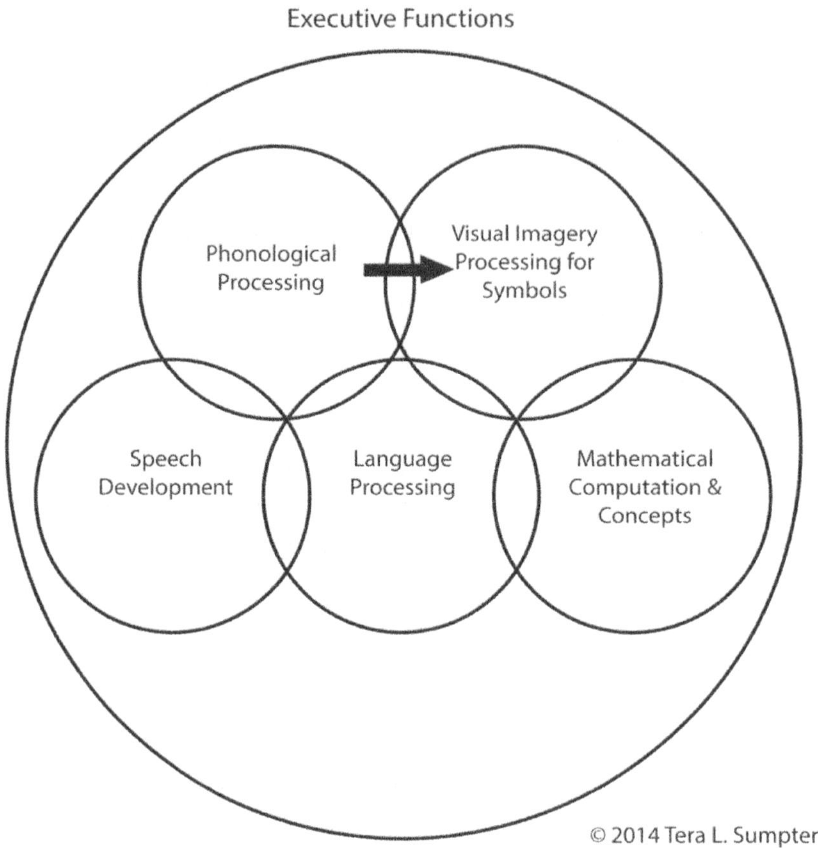

reading mechanics, do activities that strengthen reading mechanics. If you want to strengthen language, do language activities. But you won't be able to strengthen reading mechanics by using language tools.

In education today, there is a push to determine the "type" of learner that a child is. In other words, we try to determine where a child's strengths are. If he is a visual learner, we provide him with lots of visual information. If he is an auditory learner, we provide him with lots of auditory information.

This approach is a crutch.

It is a bandage.

In order to help our struggling learners effectively, we must strengthen the area of weakness, not teach to the strength.

Let me say that again for the folks in the back: **In order to help our struggling learners effectively, we must strengthen the area of weakness, not teach to the strength.**

Literacy Intervention

When deciding on a literacy intervention approach for your clients, you must first have completed a comprehensive evaluation to determine the area of cognitive weakness and level of breakdown. Once you have that information, choosing the appropriate intervention should be simple. If the area of cognitive weakness is in the phonological processing domain, you will select an intervention that stimulates phonological processing or phonemic awareness. If the area of cognitive deficit is in the visual imagery for symbols processing domain, then you will use an intervention that stimulates that area of development.

Here's the important part: **The intervention you use must start *at or before* the level of breakdown.** Many literacy interventions assume stability at 3 sounds (CVC) or 3 to 4 letters. If your student's breakdown is at the 1- or 2-sound or -letter level, your intervention beginning at 3 sounds will not be effective. The good news is that there is no shortage of literacy interventions on the market, but they must be used in a way that makes sense.

School Subjects

School is often viewed from the standpoint of content, or the material being taught. But academic learning can also be viewed from a cognitive perspective. What cognitive processing is required of a brain to learn English, math, social studies, science, or a foreign language? Our cognitive processing model (Figure 4.4) can aid us with this new vantage point.

Figure 4.4 Cognitive Processing Model

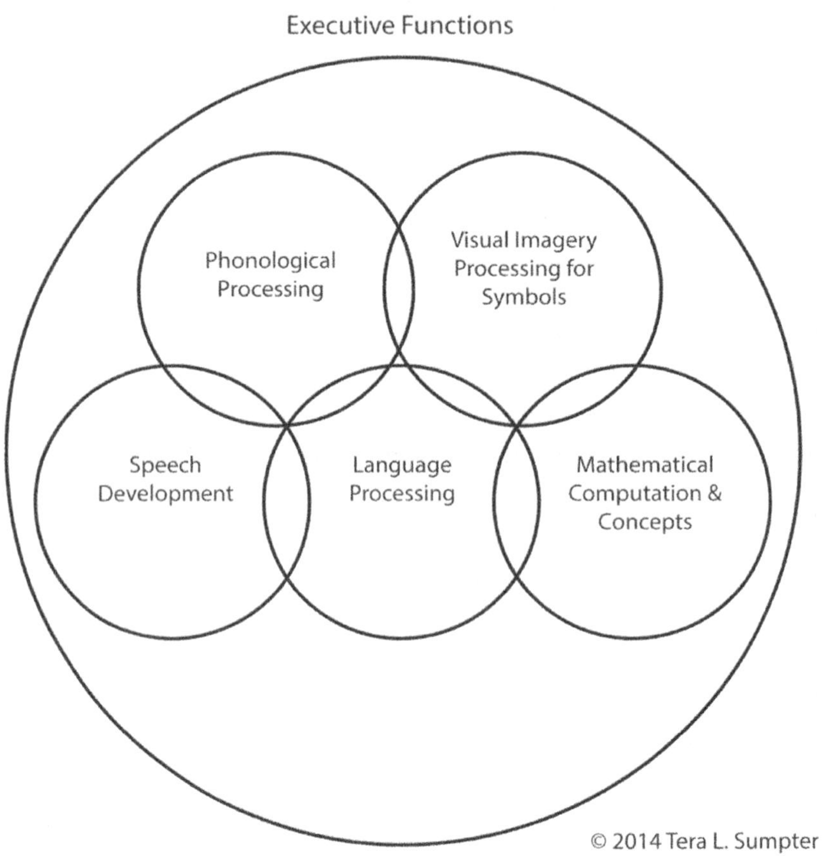

Most academic subjects require strength in all cognitive processing domains. **English/language arts** has a heavy demand on reading and writing, thereby requiring speech processing (for verbal communicators), phonological processing, visual imagery for symbols, language processing, and executive functioning.

Math demands strength in visual imagery for symbols (numbers and math symbols), language processing, and executive functioning. The executive functioning demand in math is significant. Math requires large amounts of cognitive planning and organization. In the past, children who struggled with language and literacy often still performed well in math because it was heavily focused on computation (visual imagery for symbols processing). However, with the new approaches to math, the language demand has significantly increased. As a result, many of our students who struggle in English/language arts are also struggling in math.

Science and social studies require cognitive strength in speech processing (for verbal communicators), phonological processing (PP), visual imagery for symbols (VIPS), language processing (LP), and executive functioning. PP, VIPS, and LP are all required for reading, comprehension, and verbal/written expression.

Foreign languages require the cognitive use of speech processing (for verbal communicators), phonological processing, visual imagery for symbols, language, and executive functioning. A foreign language poses an interesting demand on cognition in the form of a new phonological system: A new sound system is introduced with a new language. For children who have deficits in phonological processing, taking a foreign language can be extremely difficult.

The introduction of **cursive writing** makes its own unique demands on a student's cognition. Cursive writing is an entirely new symbol set. Therefore, children who have weakness with visual imagery for symbols processing often have a difficult time acquiring cursive.

The executive functioning demands for academic learning are immense. I will not attempt to tackle this topic here in this book, but a future book will be focused solely on executive functioning and executive functioning intervention. What I will say now is that, from waking up in the morning until going to bed at night, a child must self-regulate. She must remember to complete and turn in homework; repeatedly shift attention from the teacher to the board and then to her paper; inhibit the need for movement and exercise to sustain attention beyond her developmental capacity; integrate four cognitive domains for the purpose of reading; and use her strong working memory capacity for writing. A child's executive functioning system must be adequately developed and fully functioning all day every day for academic success. But this functioning is not happening for many of our students. The cognitive demands placed on our students today in academic settings often far exceed their developmentally appropriate executive functioning abilities.

5
Assessment

Assessment is a dynamic process. It should be viewed as a puzzle that the professional is trying to solve, a process of discovering patterns. It is not standard scores. It is not percentiles. It should not be used with the intention of landing on a diagnostic label. Instead, it is uncovering patterns of cognitive processing and performance.

For this reason, a comprehensive integrative approach must be used. One assessment typically does not provide enough information to find patterns of processing. A deep dive into each cognitive domain is needed to determine strengths and weaknesses in processing. Both receptive and expressive components of a cognitive processing domain should be examined. As discussed earlier, receptive and expressive routes in the brain are not on the same cognitive pathway. We need to examine both routes in order to get a full picture.

The key to a good assessment tool is that it isolates and measures as few cognitive processes as possible. For example, an effective phonemic awareness tool should only measure phonemic awareness. It shouldn't measure speech (i.e., the child has to say something), visual imagery for symbols (i.e., the child has to use letters or words to complete the assessment), or abstract and lengthy language (i.e., the child has to understand complex directions). All assessments, however, do require the use of self-regulation, and so all do measure executive functioning. More on that later.

Many phonemic awareness assessments look like this: Say /pat/. Now say /pat/ without saying /p/. There are some major problems with using a tool like this for phonemic awareness. First, it requires speech production. So now we're measuring speech.

Second, it requires complex language to make sense of the term "without." Now we're measuring how well the child understands a complex term. Third, we're requiring a large working memory (executive functioning) load, in that the child must hold the word, process the direction, hold the direction in working memory, and then ideally still have the word stored in phonological working memory to execute the direction. This simple task measures speech, phonemic awareness, language, and executive functioning, much more than just phonemic awareness.

So what makes up a good phonemic awareness assessment tool? It should require no speech production, no reading, and no complex directions. Make sense? If not, email me. The key is to pick assessment tools that isolate and measure as few cognitive domains as possible so that you can clearly determine the deficit area.

Table 5.1 outlines the necessary assessment tools needed for a comprehensive evaluation.

Table 5.1 Cognitive Domains and Associated Assessment Tools

COGNITIVE DOMAIN	Speech Processing	Phonological Processing	Visual Imagery Processing for Symbols	Language Processing	Executive Functioning
ASSESSMENT TOOLS	Articulation assessment	Phonemic awareness	Visual imagery for symbols	Receptive language	Parent and teacher rating scale
	Oral mechanism exam	Phonics	Sight word acquisition	Expressive language	Observation
	Conversatio nal sample	Nonsense word reading	Orthographic spelling	Writing sample	Task planning
	Diadochokin esis	Nonsense word spelling			

See Appendix B for a list of the actual assessment tools I use.

Speech Processing Assessment

You may have noticed the inclusion of diadochokinesis (DDK) in Table 5.1. Sometimes during an evaluation, you will have a student who has "phased out" or "graduated" from speech therapy or never received speech therapy at all, and this student will struggle with DDK. Does this mean the student needs speech therapy? Usually, no. More often, DDK performance can be an indicator of how that child's phonological processing system has developed and organized. I have seen over and over in my career that the breakdown level of DDK (1 sound in isolation, /p-p-p/; 2 sounds, /p-t-p-t/; or 3 sounds, /p-t-k/) corresponds with the level of phonological breakdown in phonemic awareness (single syllable phonological breakdown, /p-p-p/ DDK difficulty; 2-syllable phonological breakdown, /p-t-p-t/ DDK difficulty; or 3+ syllables phonological breakdown, /p-t-k/ DDK difficulty). Do I make a diagnosis from this information? No. It is just an extra piece in my puzzle.

When I present my cognitive model to audiences, I share an audio clip of a fifth grader who presented with significant literacy deficits. He had severely impaired phonological processing difficulties that caused a reading disorder. He had received speech therapy throughout preschool and elementary school. His speech was completely intelligible to an unknown listener, with no remarkable articulation issues. If I hadn't received a case history on him, I would not have known he had ever needed speech therapy. But his DDK was a disaster. He struggled at every single level coordinating his mouth movements. When I play the audio clip at conferences and seminars, I love watching the attendees' mouths hit the floor when they hear him.

With therapy, this student's articulation had improved, but his ability to process and coordinate sound had not. I suspect he had undiagnosed childhood apraxia of speech. Obviously, I had more information than just DDK to help me arrive at the conclusion, but it was more anecdotal than anything. I wasn't going to be treating childhood apraxia of speech anyway, so knowing about it didn't really matter other than to offer one more piece to his puzzle. He was a classic case of early speech disorder poorly wiring phonological processing and thus causing a literacy impairment.

Phonological Processing Assessment

I use four measures in my phonological processing assessment: phonemic awareness, phonics, nonsense word decoding, and nonsense word spelling.

A phonemic awareness assessment tool should examine sound manipulation at all phonemic levels: sounds in isolation, sounds in syllables beginning at 2 sounds, and multisyllables. An effective phonemic awareness measure should not involve speech production or letter recognition and should require as minimal language and executive functioning as possible.

ASSESSMENT NOTES: *Phonological Processing*

Note that the phonics, nonsense word reading, and nonsense word spelling assessment tools are also measuring visual imagery for symbols since the child is using letters. As a result, you might see issues with letter reversals. These errors are more of an indication of a child's VIPS than of phonological processing.

Also note that a hearing assessment needs to be a part of any comprehensive speech or phonological processing evaluation. You must determine whether hearing is involved in the sound (phonological) processing deficits that you are seeing.

A phonics inventory is a good measure to see how a child is processing sounds in isolation. Does the letter "p" say /pu/? I sure hope not! Is there a pattern there of epenthesis? Is the child able to isolate consonant and vowel sounds or does he combine them with vowels into CV syllables? Does he have difficulty recalling sounds?

A nonsense word reading measure should scaffold sounds from CV/VC syllables to multisyllable words. This measure should give you an indication of where the child's phonological breakdown level is. Is she able to read CV/VC and CVC words with considerable accuracy but consistently struggles at CCVC/CVCC and higher words? Look for the pattern!

A nonsense word spelling measure will be your expressive component of this cognitive domain. How does the child perform when he has to hold a word, recall the letters (symbols) that match that sound, and sequence the sounds? Look for the pattern of breakdown. Just like the nonsense word reading measure, this tool should scaffold as well. The nonsense word spelling tool I use is one I created. It is attached as Appendix C.

Visual Imagery Processing for Symbols Assessment

I use three measures in my visual imagery for symbols processing assessment: visual processing of symbols, sight words, and orthographic spelling.

To assess visual imagery for symbols, you want to have an assessment measure that shows you how many letters a child can retain and recall from visual memory. This will provide you with information on the strength of this processing area and about what level the breakdown occurs if there is one.

A sight word measure should be used to assess a student's sight word development, as this is a skill that develops from visual imagery for symbols processing.

An orthographic spelling tool should be used to assess the expressive component of this cognitive domain. This spelling measure should include words that "do not play fair": words that are not phonetic in nature, such as "know," "is," and "of." Phonetic words assess phonological processing. Orthographic words, words that you just simply have to store a picture of in your mind, are stored and assessed using visual imagery for symbols processing. In theory, you'd like this measure also to scaffold from 2-letter words to 3-letter words, and so on. But I'll be honest: I have yet to find a standardized spelling measure that only assesses orthographic spelling words and scaffolds. If you know of one, please let me know!

ASSESSMENT NOTES: ***Visual Imagery for Symbols Processing***

Please note that a vision assessment needs to be a part of any comprehensive learning or visual processing evaluation. You must determine whether vision is involved in the visual imagery processing deficits that you are seeing.

Language Processing Assessment

All of my fellow speech-language pathology warriors out there should have this area nailed down pretty well. You want to use receptive language and expressive language assessment tools. In theory, you want a scaffolded tool that shows you where a child's language breakdown occurs in both length and complexity (abstraction).

What am I analyzing in a language evaluation? I am determining whether a child has difficulty comprehending abstract language versus concrete language. I am examining whether she has difficulty comprehending lengthy amounts of language versus shorter amounts of language.

ASSESSMENT NOTES: *Language Processing*

Please note that if you're assessing reading comprehension, you always want to do a companion oral language comprehension assessment. For me, that tool is *Understanding Spoken Paragraphs* (USP) from the CELF-5. If a child does well on USP but poorly on reading comprehension, then I can be pretty confident that the reading comprehension deficit is due to the reading mechanics (phonological processing or visual imagery for symbols processing) rather than language. On the other hand, if a child does poorly on both oral language comprehension and reading comprehension, then I can conclude that there is a language deficit impacting both oral comprehension and reading comprehension.

Also note that receptive language should always be higher than expressive language. We cannot use something expressively that we do not have stored receptively. Sometimes children will present with significantly flip-flopped scores showing that expressive language is considerably higher than receptive language. Let this be an indication of potential executive functioning issues. More on that in the Executive Functioning Assessment section up next.

Executive Functioning Assessment

Standardized assessments are not good measures of executive functioning. They are too narrow and do not encompass the full scope of the executive functioning system. Dawson and Guare write in their book *Executive Skills in Children and Adolescents,* "Test scores, in and of themselves, do not provide this information [evidence of planning, organization, ability to sustain attention, impulse control] and to expect, therefore, that formal test data alone will yield definitive answers regarding executive skills deficits is a mistake" (Dawson & Guare, 2018).

A dynamic assessment approach is best for this cognitive system. My executive functioning assessment includes a parent/teacher questionnaire, a parent/teacher rating scale, extensive observation, and a work sample analysis.

To begin, when I send initial case history paperwork to a family, I include the executive functioning questionnaire. If that questionnaire comes back remarkable for EF concerns, I send a full rating scale. See Appendix D for my EF questionnaire.

Using parent and teacher rating scales is an effective way to gather significant information about a child's executive functioning abilities at home and in the classroom. George McCloskey is my preferred researcher on the topic of executive functioning. His scale, the McCloskey Executive Functions Scale (MEFS), is what I use. As shown in Appendix F, it provides information on each skill cluster of the executive functioning system.

Client observation is another key component of an EF assessment. During my comprehensive evaluations, I keep an EF skill cluster sheet with me and take copious notes on every EF skill I observe during the entire assessment process. For example, after two minutes of the assessment, a child might ask me how much longer it will be (impulsivity, pacing). He might rush through every assessment measure (self-monitoring, self-correction, impulsivity, pacing). He might be constantly yawning (energy). Maybe he cannot wait until I say, "Go" on an assessment (impulsivity, working memory, planning). He might tap the book too hard and knock it over by accident when pointing to pictures (self-modulation). Maybe he talks really loudly and has a harsh vocal quality (self-modulation). As you can imagine, I couldn't possibly list every single example here. But the point is that client observation will provide you with enormous amounts of information on a student's EF system. If you have the luxury of doing an in-home or classroom observation of your student, then DO IT!

The last tool I use for EF assessment is high-demand executive functioning tasks like alphabetizing and crossing out. These types of activities require large amounts of planning and self-regulation. When a student is completing these, I am observing and taking notes. Did she start in the middle of the page? Does she have a plan/system for how to complete the task? Is she just jumping all over the paper? Is there any organization to execution? Does she get frustrated and stop or problem solve and finish? These are all of the types of EF skills I'm assessing while the client completes the task.

ASSESSMENT NOTES: *Executive Functioning*

Please note that students with EF difficulties often perform better on expressive tasks than on receptive tasks. Why would this be? Receptive activities require significantly more self-regulation to sustain attention. Engaging activities like those that are expressive (e.g., writing, talking) are easier to attend to because we are actively engaged. But, as discussed earlier, we know that receptive skill performance should be higher than expressive skill performance. When we see the pattern of higher expressive skill performance, it should be an indicator of potential executive functioning deficits.

ASSESSMENT NOTES: *Executive Functioning* cont.

We can also conclude that, in actuality, the receptive skill abilities are higher than performance indicated. We may see these patterns across numerous cognitive domains.

Also note that if a child presents with EF difficulties, all subsystem performance may be impacted as well. Since EF regulates all of cognition, if the EF system is significantly impaired, we may see deficits across all cognitive domains. Given the assessment information we've gathered, we have to make a clinical decision on what came first, the EF impairment or the subsystem deficits. They are always connected.

Finally, please note that we are always evaluating executive functioning. There is no assessment tool that we can give that does not measure executive functioning. A child (or adult) must always use executive functioning skills to complete a task. This is important to remember when we examine performance on any and all assessments. Did the child do poorly because his phonological processing is weak, or did he perform poorly because his sustained attention is limited? Was the child's language assessment below average because of poor language development or because he has poor self-monitoring and self-correcting skills? As practitioners, we must determine what came first, the chicken or the egg. What is the underlying root cause of the deficits that you're seeing?

Literacy Assessment

As discussed in Chapter 4, literacy development is a complex network of cognitive functioning. It involves speech processing, phonological processing, visual imagery for symbols processing, language processing, and executive functioning. A thorough literacy evaluation must be utilized to make an effective and accurate literacy diagnosis. So what does this mean? A literacy evaluation must assess speech, language, phonological processing, visual imagery processing for symbols, and executive functioning—in other words, every aspect of assessment that we have already covered in this chapter.

There is one additional assessment measure that I use for literacy, and that is a contextual reading tool. It is a measure that has the child read a passage out loud and answer questions. This assessment tool allows me to gauge how well a child is **synthesizing** the literacy network of speech, phonological processing, language, visual imagery for symbols, and executive functioning. This tool also allows me to measure a child's reading rate, reading accuracy, reading fluency, and reading comprehension. As listed in Table 4.1, reading rate and reading fluency are functions of visual imagery for symbols processing, reading accuracy is a function of phonological processing, and reading comprehension is a function of language processing. Therefore, a child's reading rate and fluency should correlate with her visual imagery for symbols assessments. Her reading accuracy scores should correlate with her phonological processing domain assessments. Lastly, her reading comprehension should correlate with her language assessments. If executive functioning is a major weakness for a child, you may see inconsistency across the board.

ASSESSMENT NOTES: *Literacy*

Please note that if a child has significantly higher oral language comprehension performance than reading comprehension, this should be an indication that his reading mechanics (phonological

ASSESSMENT NOTES: *Literacy* cont.

processing and visual imagery for symbols processing) are impacting his ability to comprehend.

Also note that, in the contextual reading assessment, reading accuracy should match a child's reading comprehension. If she can read it, I want her to be able to understand it. So if a child's reading accuracy is at the 16th percentile, I want her reading comprehension to at least be at the 16th percentile as well. When reading comprehension is considerably below reading accuracy, I will be concerned about an underlying language deficit.

Finally, note that a 1-minute screening is not enough to diagnose a literacy deficit.

Written Language Assessment

Writing is by far the most complex form of expression. It involves all aspects of our cognitive model (minus math), in addition to fine motor and gross motor skills.

Obtaining a writing sample is an important part of a child's comprehensive evaluation. There are many standardized writing assessments on the market that you may use. I have always used an informal measure that provides an open-ended response. I prefer this method since it shows me a child's most natural writing.

I give the child a prompt and ask him to write as much as he can for ten minutes. Some prompts I use include the following: (1) Do you think animals belong in the circus? Yes or No. Explain your answer. (2) Tell me about the best day you ever had. (3) Tell me all about your favorite toy.

When I analyze the writing sample, I am looking for a main idea, supporting details, conclusion, thought organization, transitions, grammar, sentence length, capitalization, punctuation, and spelling.

Look for the patterns. The performance that you see on a child's writing sample should correlate with performance on the cognitive domain assessments that you administered. Main idea, supporting details, conclusion, thought organization, grammar, and sentence-length errors could all be the results of language and/or executive functioning weakness. Errors in capitalization and punctuation could be results of deficits in visual imagery for symbols processing or executive functioning. Errors in spelling could result from weaknesses in phonological processing, visual imagery for symbols processing, or executive functioning.

Children with executive functioning deficits often demonstrate considerable difficulties with writing, in particular the generation of ideas, sentence length, organization of ideas, and editing.

ASSESSMENT NOTES: *Written Language*

Please note that if you want to be the rockstar educator or clinician that I know you are, go the extra mile and show the writing sample to an occupational therapist. Oftentimes, a good OT will be able to provide you a lot of feedback and potentially the need for an OT referral from seeing a child's writing sample. Want to be even more awesome? Snap a picture of the child's pencil grasp to show the OT.

Math Assessment

Since the development of mathematics skills is acquired from the cognitive processing domains of visual imagery for symbols, language, and executive functioning, assessing those three cognitive domains often yields enough information. Rarely do children have deficits in just mathematics. Those three cognitive domains are also involved in literacy development, which is why we may see an overlap in learning disabilities. It is also why, if we strengthen the underlying cognitive weaknesses, we can improve both literacy and math at the same time.

ASSESSMENT NOTES: *Math*

An effective mathematics assessment should measure both computation and word problem skills. You should look to see if there are number reversals or difficulty with math signs (potential indication of visual imagery for symbols weakness). Look for difficulties with mathematical concepts like "greater than" or "less than" (possible language concerns). Also take note of the organization of columns and planning execution of multistep problems like long division (potential indication of executive functioning deficits).

Also note that if a child has a deficit in mathematics, you should look for an impairment in either visual imagery for symbols processing, language processing, or executive functioning or a combination of any of those.

Summary

Once we have discovered the patterns of cognitive processing weakness, then we know where and how to begin intervention. Let's continue to remind ourselves that assessment is a dynamic process of uncovering patterns of cognitive processing. Standard scores and percentiles may aid us in that pursuit; however, they will not provide us the key answer about the level at which a cognitive processing deficit is occurring. Dig into the data. Find the patterns.

As you've probably figured by now, the way I make a diagnosis is a bit different from traditional methods. My goal is to figure out the root cause of the deficits a child is displaying. We have to determine to the best of our ability which deficit(s) is (are) driving the other weaknesses. Are the language deficits the root cause of the reading impairment? Or are the reading deficits caused by weak visual imagery for symbols processing? Or maybe the child's executive functioning system is so underdeveloped that he has difficulty self-monitoring, self-correcting, and pacing himself when he reads, and that is the underlying cause of the reading impairment. Your comprehensive assessment should provide those answers.

So what would a diagnosis look like under this model? The primary diagnosis will be the root cause deficit, the weakest processing that is impacting other development. The secondary and possibly tertiary diagnoses will be the "symptom" deficits, meaning the disorders or delays that are a result of the primary weakness.

Of course, it is possible to have unrelated deficits, but this is rare as all elements of cognition function together. There is typically a driving impairment causing other deficit areas.

6
The Cognitive Ladder: Intervention Implications

Now that we have a cognitive-based holistic approach to examine the deficits with which a child is presenting, we need to consider the implications for intervention.

Let's consider the term *cognitive ladder* (see Figure 6.1). The cognitive ladder is the systematic progression of cognitive load

Figure 6.1 The Cognitive Ladder

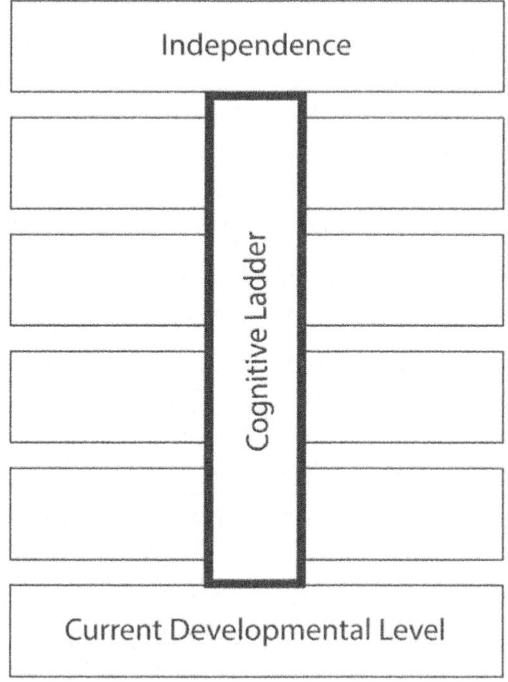

tasks that start at a child's current developmental level, end in independence, and contain a progressive sequence of steps to build cognitive processing skills. The end goal of independence is obviously going to look different for each child.

This type of systematic sequential progressive load should be able to be applied to any aspect of cognitive therapy: speech, language, literacy, or executive functioning. The key to an effective cognitive ladder is that each step builds on the one before it. I can't lift 20 pounds before I can lift 5 pounds, and I can't run before I can walk. Similarly, a baby will typically coo before he babbles, and he is going to babble before he uses full words. Children will typically use single words to communicate, then two words, and next short phrases until they're speaking in full sentences. There are certain abilities that must be done in a sequential progressive fashion, and cognitive development should not be viewed any differently.

A popular type of language therapy is theme-based activities. In October, for example, you might do Fall or Halloween activities, or the month of April might bring Spring-based tasks about leaves and flowers. I would challenge everyone doing this kind of therapy to determine where in the cognitive ladder these activities fit. Are we simply exposing children to vocabulary and concepts or are we wiring their cognition to be able to acquire these vocabulary concepts on their own? If the activity is targeting language from an increased length and complexity manner, then I'd support its use. If it is being used simply for exposure to new vocabulary and concepts, I would suggest rethinking its implementation.

How does this idea of a cognitive ladder apply to our cognitive processing model? If we determine that a child's phonological processing breakdown level is 2 sounds, then we would start therapy at the 1- or 2-sound level and build up to 3 sounds, 4 sounds, 5 sounds, and so on until she is independent at an appropriate level. If we find that a child's visual processing for symbols breaks down at the 4-letter level, then we would start therapy at the 3- to 4-letter level, move to 5 letters, 6 letters, 2 syllables, 3 syllables, and so on until she is independent at an appropriate level.

Language therapy is a bit more complicated because there are so many moving pieces and parts. But we need to stay focused on addressing a child's connection to the length and complexity of language rather than feeling the need to address every little language skill (e.g., past tense *-ed, wh-* questions, third person singular).

Now I know you're all thinking, "What?! That's it for therapy? Tera, give me the therapy!" I will. It's coming. I can't tackle all of that here (or this book would never get finished). But I wanted to leave you with a framework for identifying impairments in cognitive processing deficits so we have a better way to identify struggling learners and then provide a progressive sequential context for therapy.

The key to good therapy begins with assessment. We have to know what we're looking at before we can decide on the right treatment protocol. My subsequent books will apply these theories to various therapy topics like executive functioning and language. So hang tight. It's coming.

7
Client Reports

In Chapters 2 and 3, we examined client reports about a single cognitive deficit. It is rarely the case that just one cognitive weakness is present in a client profile. In this chapter, we will examine client reports more typically seen in clinical practice, ones that are more complex in nature and in which multiple systems of cognition are impacted and multiple deficits are connected.

This book is intended primarily to be a diagnostic manual for the practitioner. For that reason, we outline the diagnostics of the clients in this chapter but we do not address therapy outcomes. Therapy progression, application, and outcomes will be discussed in subsequent books. Please note that all of the children discussed in this chapter made significant gains over the course of their treatment.

The diagrams included are intended to provide a visual representation of the clients' deficits. The diagram serves as the first page of my evaluation report. I enter the child's scores in the appropriate circles and highlight deficit areas in thicker lines so that they are easy to see.

Client Report 1: Mateo

History

- Chronological age: 6-1
- Grade level: repeating kindergarten
- He is receiving OT for low-performing vestibular system and child psychology for flexible thinking and behavior.
- His emotions lead to anxiety regarding parent separation.

- He lacks interest in brushing hair and teeth (fights and screams).
- He puts his hands over his ears when he doesn't want to talk about something.
- He enjoys hours of innovation and creative play (e.g., Lego building).

Chief Complaint

- Mateo is experiencing frustration and unwillingness to try to develop words (in relation to reading).
- Caregivers noticed the issue at the beginning of kindergarten.
- Mateo's kindergarten teacher completed the CELF-5 Observational Rating Scale for him. She reports that Mateo often has trouble paying attention. Additionally, she partially completed the McCloskey Executive Functions Scale (MEFS) and reported that Mateo seldom does the following on his own without being prompted, reminded, or cued:
  - waits for his turn
  - maintains emotional control when disagreeing with peers
  - returns to a school task after a pause
  - pauses to listen to others
  - returns to what he was thinking about after a pause
  - tries a different way to complete a task when stuck
  - accepts a good idea when it is what most of a group wants to do
  - accepts changes in school or routine without getting upset
  - moves from one school task or social activity to another without difficulty
  - checks his work to avoid errors
  - recognizes when his behavior upsets others
  - checks to make sure he has what he needs before leaving class
  - checks his appearance and personal hygiene.

- She also reported that Mateo only does the following tasks after being prompted, reminded, or cued:
    - focuses attention on school tasks
    - considers the consequences before saying or doing things he may regret
    - refrains from acts of physical aggression
    - knows when to stop talking about a single topic
    - stops playing a game or desired task when asked
    - stops doing harmful or bothersome things to himself when asked
    - changes personal habits when they are causing problems
    - modulates his physical activity level to fit the situation of school tasks and working in a group
    - adjusts physical activity when working alone
    - modulates his emotions to fit the situation when working on school tasks and with others
    - avoids being over- or understimulated by sights, sounds, or touches.
- Mateo stops doing things that annoy others after being asked to do so only when he has direct assistance.

Client Presentation

- lots of yawning (energy)
- grabbing all objects on table (inhibition, stopping)
- counting number of stickers (inhibition, self-monitoring, self-correction)
- comments that short tasks feel long (pacing, time sense)
- has difficulty repeating short sound sequences like /b/-/b/-/z/ (focus, sustained attention, phonological [verbal] working memory)
- has difficulty recalling previously seen letter sequences and words (focus, sustained attention, visual or nonverbal working memory)

- demonstrates good critical thinking

Assessment Outcome

Mateo is a creative young boy. Mateo has many cognitive strengths, including understanding language for following directions and relationships among language concepts.

Mateo presents with age-appropriate receptive and expressive language skills. However, it should be noted that there is almost a 1 standard deviation range between Mateo's receptive and expressive language abilities. It is suspected that Mateo's expressive language results may have been impacted by executive function regulation during assessment completion.

Mateo presents with a reading impairment characterized by weakness in phonological processing of phonemes and visual imagery processing for symbols. His phonological processing difficulty was observed at C, V, and CV/VC phoneme levels. Mateo's visual imagery for symbols processing is characterized by decreased working memory for holding up to two visual symbols at a time. Difficulties with visual imagery processing for symbols are suspected to be impacting the development of mathematics due to its symbol system nature.

Mateo presents with weaknesses in executive functioning characterized by difficulties with focus, sustained attention, inhibition, self-monitoring, self-correcting, stopping, pacing, time sense, verbal and nonverbal working memory, and appropriate energy for tasks.

Diagnoses

1. Reading Impairment
2. Executive Function Impairment

Figure 7.1 Cognitive Processing Model for Mateo

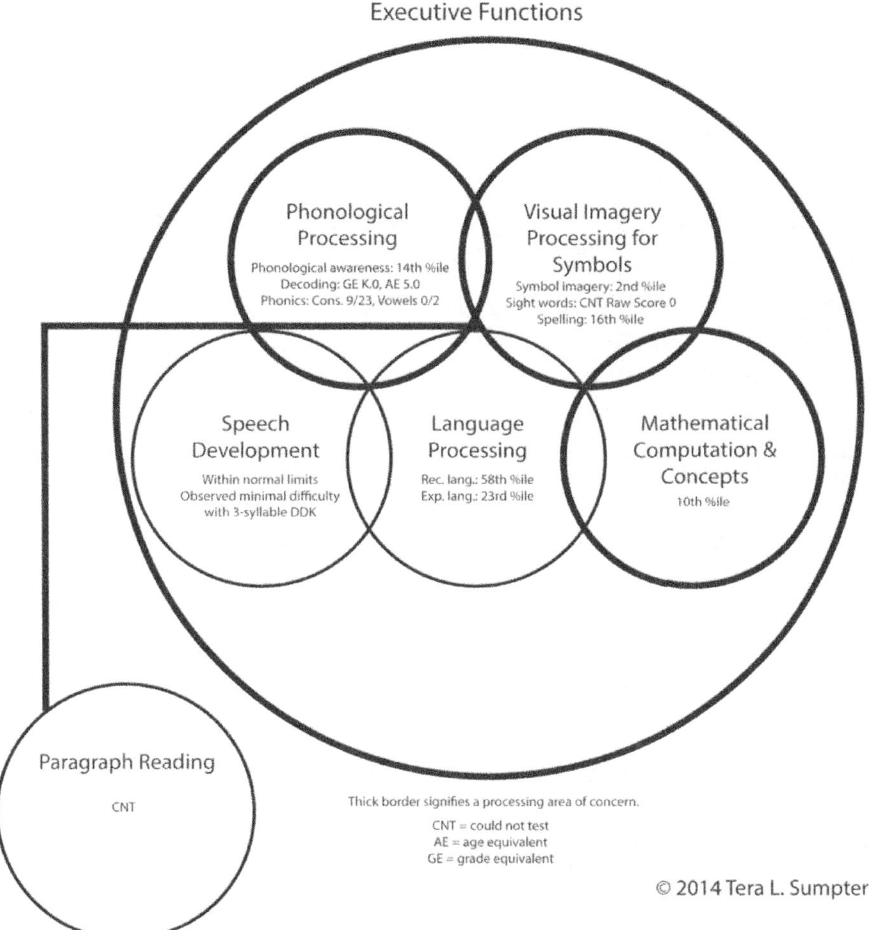

Conclusions

We were unsure if delayed academic learning was due to inability to attend or cognitive demand of academic tasks, particularly literacy. Considering Mateo's prior sensory and behavioral diagnoses, we suspected executive functioning delays, most likely causing delays in academic learning (literacy focused). Due to Mateo's young age and variability in executive functioning development at that age, executive functioning was given as the secondary diagnosis as opposed to primary.

Therapy Plan

It is recommended that Mateo receive therapy three to four times per week with a focus on developing his phonological processing and visual imagery processing for symbols for literacy and executive functioning skills. Executive functioning therapy will be used to facilitate literacy therapy.

Client Report 2: Peter

Case History

- Chronological age: 16-3
- Grade level: tenth grade
- He was born seven weeks early, weighing 4 lbs. 3 oz.
- He spent five weeks in the NICU due to low birth weight and jaundice.
- He has phenylketonuria (PKU), a rare inherited disorder that causes the amino acid phenylalanine to build up in the body. Peter's diet and phenylalanine levels have been monitored since birth, and he has been on a modified diet since.
- He has been diagnosed with ADHD, anxiety, and depression. He is currently taking Prozac (30 mg), Ritalin (10 mg), and Periflex (180 grams/daily PKU formula).
- He currently sees a counselor, psychiatrist, and metabolic specialist.
- Peter has passed hearing screenings, and he currently wears glasses.

Chief Complaint

- Parent report noted that Peter has severe difficulty staying on task, staying focused, and completing tasks on time or independently.
- He has difficulty with handwriting and avoids it at all costs.
- His handwriting is messy and not as expected for a 16 year old. This causes him not to want to write.
- He has difficulty in organizing his thoughts to translate them into cohesive sentences in written form, with this proving difficult in writing even a basic paragraph.
- Peter can read, although he no longer chooses to do so.
- The last few years he has struggled even more and has started lying obsessively and avoiding any academic work.
- Peter's struggles were first observed when he was in kindergarten.
- He has been on an Individualized Education Plan (IEP) since the first grade.

Client Presentation

- picking at nails
- loud, impulsive, and negative talking
- not interested in what examiner said (perception, impulsivity)
- a lot of out loud self-talk
- lots of sniffing
- lots of off-task talking
- when dumping blocks out of the box and they went all over the table and onto the floor, he was surprised (anticipation)
- didn't like writing topic given by examiner and asked for another one (flexibility)
- during writing sample, commented on church bells, dad's arrival, and the time (focus, sustained attention, impulsivity)

- during 10 minutes given for writing sample, stared at his paper for several minutes
- completed three sentences in 4 minutes
- after 6 minutes, said he was done
- after examiner prompt to write more, wrote one more sentence in 2 minutes and was done after 8 minutes (focus, sustained attention, initiation, generation)

Assessment Outcome

Peter is a kind and engaging young boy. As evidenced throughout the assessment process and noted in parent and teacher report and scales, Peter presents with severe deficits in executive functioning. He demonstrates weakness in the following executive functioning skills:

- self-awareness
- attention
- initiation
- flexibility
- self-monitoring
- self-correcting
- balancing
- gauging
- anticipating
- estimating time
- analyzing
- self-evaluation
- generating
- organization
- planning
- prioritizing
- decision-making

- time sense
- pacing
- executing routines
- storing/retrieving information

Peter's executive functioning deficits, especially his poor self-regulation skills, are significantly contributing to his overall learning struggles, in particular with reading, writing, comprehension, and math. His executive functioning weaknesses are of primary concern.

Peter presents with a reading impairment characterized by deficits in both phonological and visual imagery for symbols cognitive processing areas.

Peter presents with a language impairment characterized by deficits in written language expression, comprehension of language abstraction, and reading comprehension.

Diagnoses

1. Executive Functioning Impairment
2. Reading Impairment
3. Language Impairment

Conclusions

Peter's executive functioning deficits are significantly contributing to his reading and language impairments, as well as his difficulties with math.

Therapy Plan

Due to Peter's age, deficit complexity, and deficit severity, it is recommended that he receive therapy four times per week for hour-long sessions with a focus on developing his executive functioning skills for self-regulation, phonological and visual imagery processing for reading, and language processing for written language, language abstraction, and reading comprehension. Treatment will initially focus on Peter's executive functioning skills in isolation and then transition to a literacy-executive function integrated therapy approach when appropriate.

Figure 7.2 Cognitive Processing Model for Peter

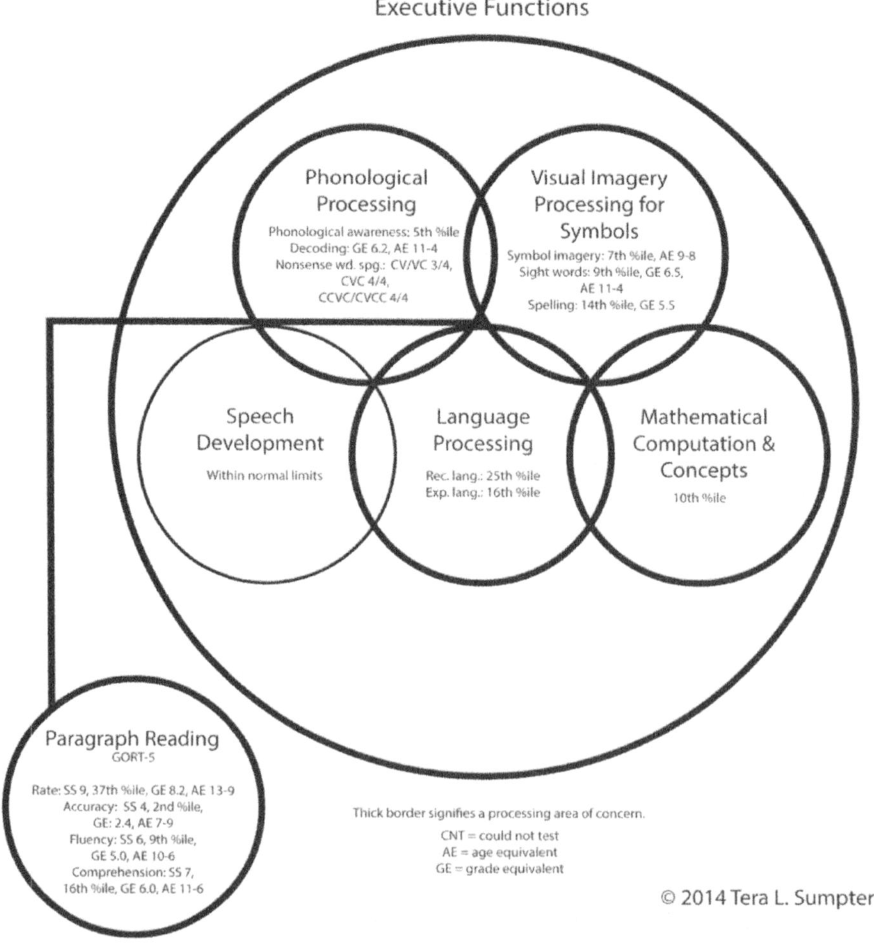

Thereafter, therapy will transition to an integrated language-executive functioning treatment approach when appropriate. Therapy will introduce executive function therapy to establish plans and routines for intervention. Once the ability to plan is established, therapy will transition to a literacy focus to stabilize reading for academic development. Executive function therapy will facilitate literacy intervention. When appropriate, therapy will transition to language intervention with an executive functioning approach. It is also recommended that Peter receive a comprehensive occupational therapy evaluation.

Client Report 3: Noah

Due to the severity of Noah's executive functioning deficits, he was unable to complete any formal testing. As a result, I did not complete a diagram for him.

Case History

- Chronological age: 7-4
- Grade level: first grade
- Mother reported a normal pregnancy and delivery.
- No accidents, hospitalizations, or trauma reported.
- Noah is reportedly a healthy, happy child.
- Noah received traditional speech-language therapy for four years with minimal progress observed.

Chief Complaint

Noah's family is concerned about his speech and language skills. He is struggling in school and had to repeat kindergarten.

Client Presentation

Throughout the evaluation, Noah was happy and playful. He needed near constant redirection to attend to assessment tasks. The CELF-5 was attempted unsuccessfully due to Noah's lack of perception, sustained attention, and inhibition. The PLS-5 was administered in an attempt to obtain a baseline performance level, but Noah could not complete it due to his lack of attention and ability to follow directions. Noah was unable to participate in conversational turn taking due to his lack of conversational perception.

Assessment Outcome

Noah presents with a severe executive functioning impairment characterized by deficits in perception, focusing, sustaining attention, shifting attention, and inhibition. These executive functioning weaknesses appear to be driving his language and articulation impairments as he is not attentionally connected to his environment.

Noah presents with a severe receptive and expressive language disorder characterized by impaired auditory comprehension and verbal expression. He demonstrates developmental gaps in the areas of pronoun comprehension and usage (e.g., I, they, he, she), age-appropriate sentence length (e.g. "play her sister," "I know eat dinner," "wear sweaters"), following verbal directions (unable to follow one-step commands independently), repeating verbal information of increasing lengths and complexities, using appropriate verb tense (no past tense verbs observed), and using irregular plural nouns. His language errors were highly inconsistent. A complete language inventory was unable to be obtained due to Noah's inability to sustain attention and follow assessment directives.

Noah presents with an articulation disorder characterized by inconsistent substitutions, distortions, and omissions of consonant sounds in words, particularly medial sound omissions. Vowel distortions were also observed. His speech errors follow no pattern and are highly inconsistent. He presents with atypical prosodic patterns as well. The following are examples of his speech errors: /noozd/ for "used," /ameedadum/ for "in the garden," and /ayo eeno dus a eeno bit/ for "you know just a little bit."

Diagnoses

1. Severe Executive Functioning Impairment
2. Severe Receptive and Expressive Language Disorder
3. Articulation Disorder

Conclusions

Noah's inability to perceive and focus on his environment and inhibit his own thoughts and desires is significantly impacting his ability to develop speech and language.

Therapy Plan

It is recommended that Noah receive speech and literacy therapy three to four times per week with an initial focus on developing his executive functioning skills of perception, focus, and inhibition during concrete desirable and undesirable tasks. When appropriate, therapy will address perception, focus, and sustained attention for simple questions and one-step directions. In addition, therapy will address simple yet complete sentence structure usage.

Client Report 4: Samara

Case History

- Chronological age: 10-1
- Grade level: fourth grade
- Mother reported a normal pregnancy.
- Mother was induced three weeks early due to developing toxemia. Delivery was difficult as forceps and a vacuum were required.
- Samara weighed 7 lbs. 3 oz. at birth and was listed in "good range" for all areas.
- Currently, Samara is a healthy child with no reported medical issues. She is currently on no medications. No food or other allergies were reported.
- Samara received private speech therapy for one year and has received school speech therapy since kindergarten. Mother reported seeing minimal progress.
- Samara has an IEP for speech. She receives 60 minutes a week of speech therapy.

Chief Complaint

Samara's parents are concerned about her speech, reading, and writing skills. On her most recent report card, she received As in math, social studies, and science; a B+ in writing; and a C+ in reading. Her mother is an elementary school teacher and has tried numerous different interventions to help Samara with her literacy skills. Her mother reported minimal success with all of those interventions.

Client Presentation

Throughout the evaluation, Samara worked hard and stayed focused for the duration of the assessment. She was quiet and cooperative and made good eye contact with the examiner.

Assessment Outcome

Samara is a sweet and hard-working individual. She has numerous cognitive strengths including her receptive and expressive language skills. Samara presents with a speech disorder characterized by the vowelization of the /r/ phoneme and /r/-blends and interdentalization of /s/ phonemes and /s/-blends in all positions of words. She demonstrates lingual weakness when protruded and lateralized. The lingual weakness is most likely contributing to her misarticulations. Samara also demonstrates mild oral apraxiclike tendencies during diadochokinetic activities and occasional conversational speech tasks, particularly with multisyllabic words.

Samara presents with a severe reading impairment characterized by deficits in both the phonological and visual imagery for symbols processing cognitive domains necessary for reading. She exhibits difficulty in phonologically processing vowel sounds, sounds in simple and complex single-syllable words, and syllables in multisyllabic words; and she shows difficulty with multisyllable encoding and decoding. Samara has impaired visual imagery for symbols as evidenced by poor retention and recall of >4-letter words and multisyllable words, poor sight word acquisition, and poor orthographic spelling.

Diagnoses

1. Severe Specific Reading Disorder
2. Speech Disorder (apraxiclike tendencies)

Figure 7.3 Cognitive Processing Model for Samara

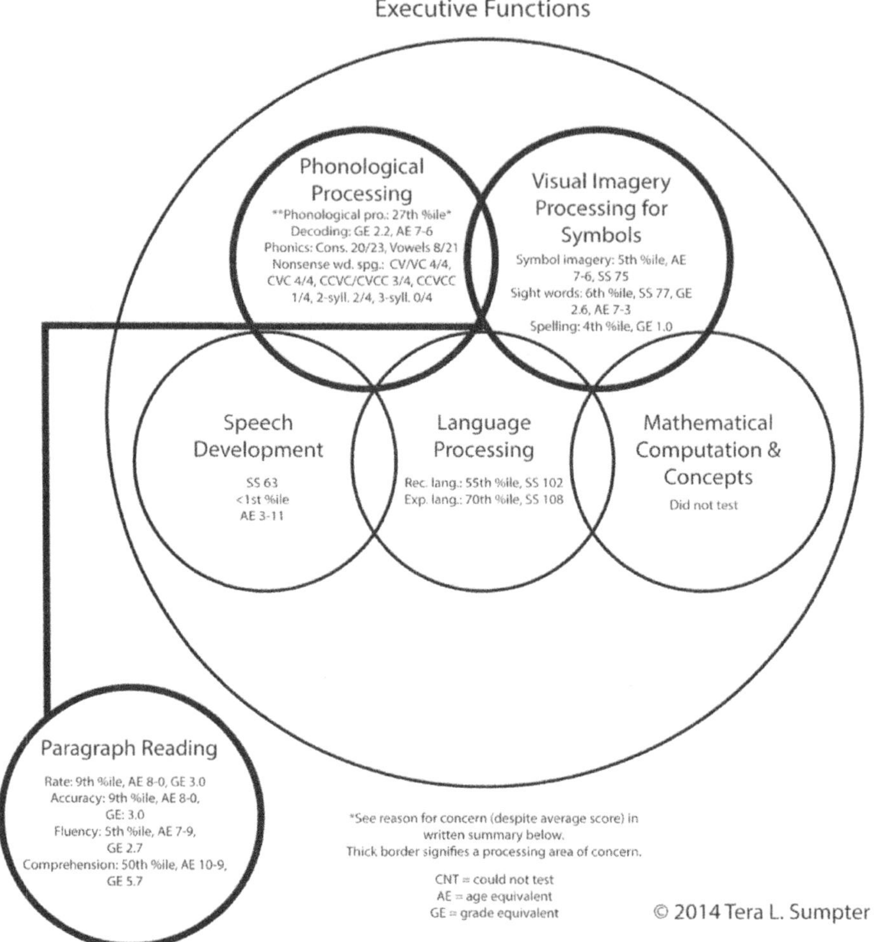

Conclusions

Therapist suspects undiagnosed and untreated childhood apraxia of speech due to poor progress with traditional speech therapy, performance on DDK, residual speech errors, difficulty coordinating multisyllable words in conversational speech, and Samara's disinterest in speaking. Samara's reading impairment is most likely a result of her residual speech disorder, which impacted her phonological processing development. Her weak visual imagery for symbols is most likely a result of her weak phonological processing.

Therapy Plan

It is recommended that Samara receive speech and literacy therapy two to three times per week with a focus on developing her phonological processing skills for reading, visual imagery for symbols (letters and numbers), and oral motor and speech abilities for the /r/ and /s/ phonemes and multisyllable words at all linguistic levels.

Client Report 5: Garret

Case History

- Chronological age: 12-5
- Grade level: seventh grade
- Mother reported a normal pregnancy.
- Garret was born full-term, weighing 8 lbs.
- Garret was born with a hole in his heart that closed on its own by the time he was 6 months old.
- He was hospitalized at 7 days for dehydration and poor eating.
- At age 1, he had surgery for PE tubes.
- Currently, Garret is a healthy child with no reported medical issues.
- He has received previous diagnoses of ADHD–inattentive type and anxiety. He takes Adderall (20 mg) once a day.
- He is allergic to pollen and grass. No known food allergies at this time.

Chief Complaint

Despite average performance in school, Garret spends a lot of time on his work expending significant effort. His mother reports that he struggles more and more with each passing school year. She knows something is wrong despite the school saying he is fine.

Client Presentation

Throughout the evaluation, Garret worked hard and stayed focused for the duration of the assessment. He was cooperative and made good eye contact with the examiner.

Assessment Outcome

Garret is a kind and engaging boy. He has many strengths including language of decreased length, literacy mechanics (phonological and visual imagery processing for symbols), and pragmatic skills. Garret presents with an executive functioning impairment characterized by deficits in the following skills clusters:

- attention
- engagement (initiating, inhibiting, stopping, shifting)
- optimization (self-monitoring, self-modulating intensity, self-correcting)
- efficiency (sensing time, pacing work, sequencing)
- working memory (holding and manipulating information in mind, storing and retrieving information)
- inquiry (gauging difficulty and resources needed, anticipating, analyzing)

- solution (generating ideas, making associations, organizing, planning, prioritizing, decision making)

These deficits are observed in both academic and self/social arenas of involvement.

On the *Seeds of Learning* Executive Function Questionnaire, Garret's mother noted that he often has difficulty with the following skills:

- paying attention
- initiating tasks
- stopping a task when asked to stop
- shifting from one task to another
- modulating his loudness level when speaking
- estimating how long a task will take
- sequencing the order of commands
- remembering information or events
- gauging his own behavior in response to someone else's behavior
- estimating what time it is
- prioritizing tasks
- making decisions
- planning out tasks
- organizing

Garret presents with a receptive language impairment characterized by deficits in comprehending oral and written language of increasing length. These deficits are most likely a result of his poor sustained attention.

Garret's vocal quality is moderately dysphonic, characterized by a raspy, breathy hoarseness.

Figure 7.4 Cognitive Processing Model for Garret

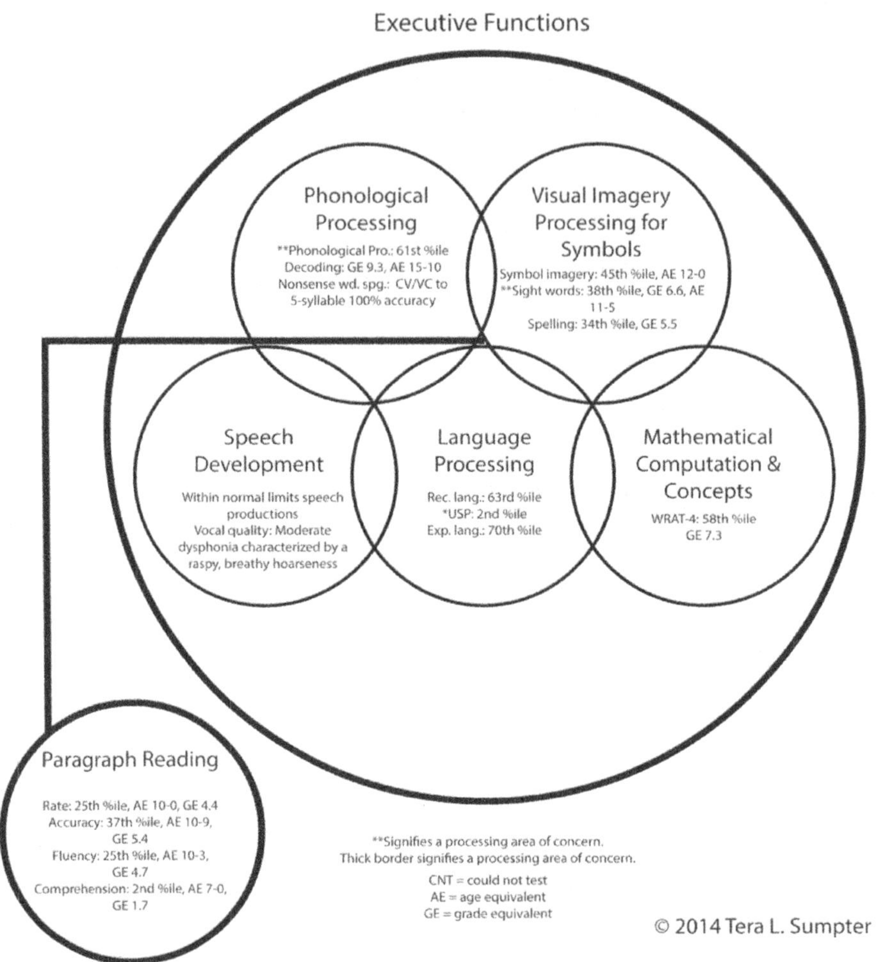

Diagnoses

1. Executive Functioning Impairment
2. Receptive Language Impairment

Conclusions

Garret's executive functioning deficits are significantly contributing to his language and reading comprehension impairments. His difficulty in self-regulating attention and planning are impacting his ability to comprehend language of increased length like short paragraphs and stories. Garret's dysphonia is most likely connected to his inability to modulate his loudness level (executive functioning) and is, as a result, causing damage to his vocal folds.

Therapy Plan

It is recommended that Garret receive therapy two to three times per week for hour-long sessions with a focus on developing his visualization for executive functioning and receptive language, reading comprehension, and written language expression. Executive functioning therapy should be integrated at all times. A voice evaluation is recommended to determine the nature and cause of his dysphonia.

Client Report 6: Carmen

Case History

- Chronological age: 8-4
- Grade level: second grade
- Mother reported a normal pregnancy.
- Carmen was born full-term, weighing 12 lbs.
- Carmen is a healthy child with no history of major accidents, illnesses, hospitalizations, or surgeries.
- She is currently not taking any medications, and no allergies to food or environmental agents were reported.

- Carmen's hearing has been tested at routine physical exams and found to be normal.

Chief Complaint

Carmen is currently homeschooled and attending an online school. Her mother reports that she struggles with reading, spelling, and writing letters correctly. Her mother has homeschooled all of Carmen's older siblings and never had difficulty teaching any of them to read and write. Despite Carmen's apparent intelligence, she is having difficulty learning these skills.

Client Presentation

Throughout the evaluation, Carmen worked hard and was cooperative. She made good eye contact with the examiner. She remained attentive and hardworking throughout the duration of this evaluation.

Assessment Outcome

Carmen has many cognitive strengths, including receptive and expressive language. Carmen's language skills are above average for age-level expectations.

Carmen presents with a mild reading impairment characterized by weakness in both phonological processing and visual imagery processing for symbols. Phonologically, Carmen has difficulty processing words at the multisyllable level. Carmen's visual imagery processing for symbols is the more significant concern as demonstrated by difficulty holding, manipulating, and retrieving letters for the purposes of sight word acquisition, spelling, and reading rate and fluency.

Diagnosis

Reading Impairment

Figure 7.5 Cognitive Processing Model for Carmen

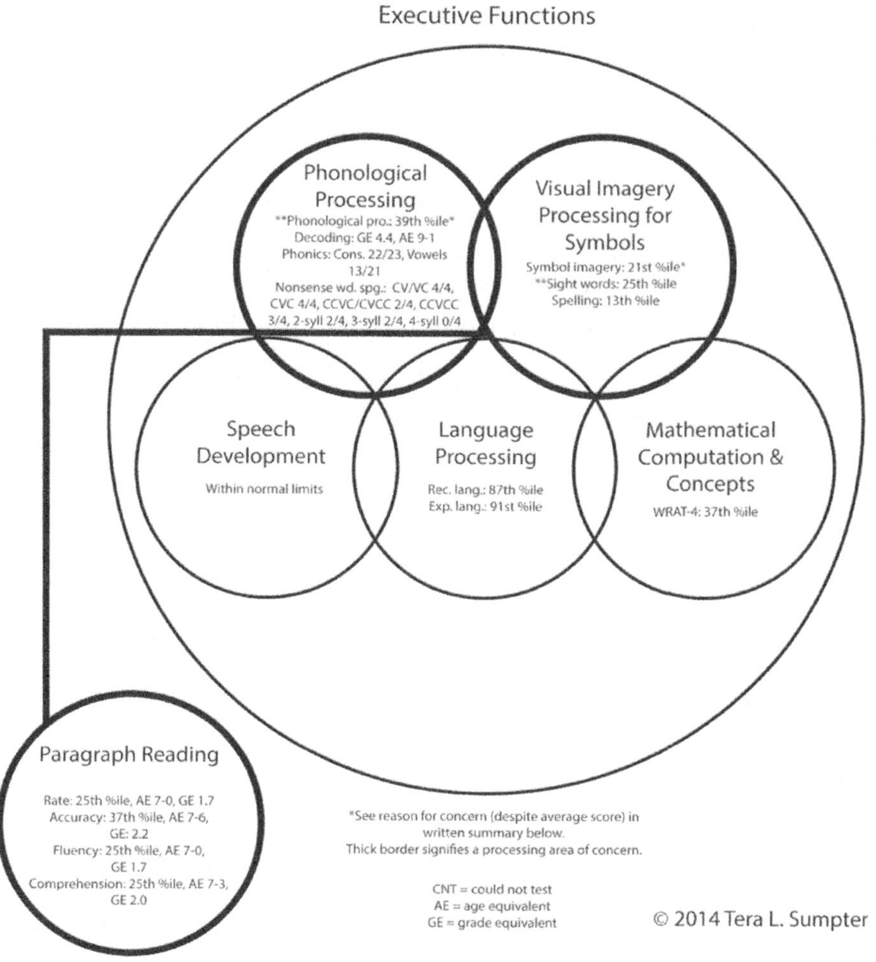

Conclusions

Despite the fact that Carmen's reading comprehension scores are technically within normal limits at the 25th percentile, these scores are considerably lower than her oral language comprehension scores. We would expect to see reading comprehension and oral language comprehension scores more consistent with one another. This discrepancy suggests that the weakness of her reading mechanics is impacting her ability to comprehend what she reads.

Carmen is a great example of how a child with high language ability can compensate for other deficits. In a school setting, she probably would not have been identified. But the large gap between her language skills and her reading comprehension was a significant red flag that there was a breakdown in processing, and our assessment located that breakdown in the visual processing for symbols area.

Therapy Plan

It is recommended that Carmen receive literacy therapy two to three times per week for 60-minute sessions with a focus on developing her phonological processing and visual imagery processing of symbols for literacy development.

Afterword

I hope this book has been eye-opening. I hope it has provided you with a new framework to assess and view impairments in your struggling learners, a framework that is cognitive-based and holistic. I know you want the therapy, and I am so appreciative of your patience.

Feel free to reach out and let me know if there's anything in particular you would like me to address in subsequent books. You can find me on Instagram at @terasumpter_slp, where I frequently share education and therapy ideas, or reach me via email at tera@seedsoflearningllc.com.

Thank you for joining me on this journey outside the box.

Appendices

Appendix A
Syllable Structure Examples

cv/vc	go/up
cvc	cup
ccv/vcc	spy/ask
ccvc/cvcc	stop/must
ccvcc	ground
cccvcc	stretched
2-syllable	nation
3-syllable	convention
4-syllable	ability
5-syllable	refrigerator
6-syllable	capitalization
7-syllable	inevitability

Appendix B
Assessment Tool List

Speech	*Goldman Fristoe Test of Articulation—Third Edition (GFTA-3)*

Phonological Processing	
Phonemic awareness	*Lindamood Auditory Conceptualization Test—Third Edition (LAC-3)*
Phonics	Informal inventory Appendix E
Nonsense word phonetic reading	Word Attack subtest from the *Woodcock Reading Mastery Tests—Revised (WRMT-R)*
Nonsense word phonetic spelling	Informal inventory Appendix C

Language Processing	
Receptive Language	*Clinical Evaluation of Language Fundamentals—Fifth Edition (CELF-5)*
Expressive Language	*Clinical Evaluation of Language Fundamentals—Fifth Edition (CELF-5)*

Visual Imagery for Symbols Processing	
Visual Imagery for Symbols	*Symbol Imagery Test*
Sight Words	*Slosson Oral Reading Test—Third Edition (SORT-R3)*
Orthographic spelling	Spelling subtest of *Wide Range Achievement Test—Fifth Edition (WRAT-5)*

Paragraph Reading	*Gray Oral Reading Test—Fifth Edition (GORT-5)*

Executive Functioning	
	Seeds of Learning LLC Executive Functioning Questionnaire Appendix D
	McCloskey Executive Functions Scale (MEFS); parent and teacher rating scale
	Observation checklist Appendix F
	Worksheets from *Executive Functions Training—Adolescents* by Lynn A. Drazinski; executive functioning tasks (e.g., alphabetizing, crossing out)

Mathematics	Math subtest of *Wide Range Achievement Test—Fourth Edition (WRAT-4)*

Appendix C
Nonsense Word Spelling Assessment Measure

CV/VC

1. et
2. pi
3. goo
4. ach

CVC

5. zon
6. mave
7. pud
8. bime

CCVC/CVCC

9. stid
10. flup
11. shoost
12. luks

CCVCC

13. gribs
14. slups
15. stesk
16. frunch

2 syllable

17. tenture
18. slotion
19. pretap
20. conflip

3 syllable

21. askerness
22. siptery
23. idderly
24. exflative

4 syllable

25. amflacation
26. thisterpumble
27. moperbindly
28. retembertive

5 syllable

29. rederplatively
30. indirectionly
31. consipnotable
32. allerbaskerness

Appendix D
Seeds of Learning
Executive Functioning
Questionnaire

Executive Functioning Questionnaire

Child's name: ______________________________ Age:______ Date of birth:______________ Date completed: ____________

Who completed this form? _________________________________ Relationship to child: _________________________________

	Never	Sometimes	Often	Always
Is your child aware of his/her surroundings?				
Do they seem to be in their "own world"?				
About how long can your child sustain attention to a desired task?				
About how long can your child sustain attention to an undesirable task?				
Would you characterize your child as lethargic?				
Would you characterize your child as impulsive/having difficulty inhibiting their behaviors?				
Does your child make careless mistakes on their schoolwork?				
Does your child catch their mistakes on schoolwork?				
Does your child rush through tasks?				
Does it take a long time for your child to complete tasks?				
Does your child have difficulty...				
• paying attention?				
• staying energized through structured tasks?				
• staying energized through unstructured tasks?				
• initiating tasks?				
• stopping a behavior when asked to stop?				
• shifting from one task to another?				
• with transitions?				
• sharing?				
• "going with the flow"?				
• modulating their emotions (e.g., have explosive outbursts, zip from 0-100)?				
• modulating how loud they are?				
• estimating how long an activity will take?				
• sequencing the order of commands?				
• sequencing the order of memories?				
• remembering information or events?				
• predicting what will happen next or later?				
• gauging their own behavior in response to someone else's behavior?				
• gauging how someone else may or may not respond?				
• estimating what time it is?				
• seeing relationships among objects or items (e.g., what is the same about a tire and the sun?)?				
• coming up with their own novel thoughts and ideas?				
• making associations?				
• prioritizing tasks?				
• planning out tasks or planning out their day?				
• with organization?				
• making decisions (i.e., are they indecisive?)?				

16927 Detroit Ave., Suite 5, Lakewood OH 44107 • 440-454-1686
terasumpter@seedsoflearningllc.com • www.seedsoflearningllc.com

What else should we know about your child? Please list any other concerns or observations that you have about your child.

16927 Detroit Ave., Suite 5, Lakewood OH 44107 • 440-454-1686
terasumpter@seedsoflearningllc.com • www.seedsoflearningllc.com

Appendix E
Phonics Inventory

<u>Consonants</u>

t

n

r

m

d

s

l

c

p

b

f

v

g

h

k

w

j

z

th

sh

ch

qu

ph

ng

<u>Vowels</u>

a

e

i

o

u

oo

au

aw

ee

ea

oa

ai

ay

er

ir

ur

or

ar

oi

ou

oy

ow

Appendix F
Executive Functioning Observation Checklist

This checklist is derived from the *McCloskey Executive Functions Scale (MEFS).**

ATTENTION
Perception
Focus
Sustained attention

ENGAGEMENT
Energize
Initiate
Inhibit
Stop
Pause
Flexible
Shift

OPTIMIZATION
Self-Monitor
Self-Modulate
Balance
Self-Correct

EFFICIENCY
Sense Time
Pace
Sequence
Execute

MEMORY
Hold
Manipulate
Store
Retrieve

INQUIRY
Anticipate
Gauge
Analyze
Estimate Time
Compare

SOLUTION
Generate
Associate
Prioritize
Plan
Organize
Decide

*McCloskey et al., 2009.

References

Alloway, T. P., Tewolde, F., Skipper, D., & Hijar, D. (2017). Can you spell dyslexia without SLI? Comparing the cognitive profiles of dyslexia and specific language impairment and their roles in learning. *Research in Developmental Disabilities* 65:97-102.

Alt, M., Arizmendi, G. D., & Beal, C. R. (2014). The relationship between mathematics and language: Academic implications for children with specific language impairment and English language learners. *Language, Speech, and Hearing Services in Schools* 45(3):220-233.

Aron, A. R., Robbins, T. W., & Poldrack, R. A. (2004). Inhibition and the right inferior frontal cortex. *Trends in Cognitive Sciences* 8(4):170–177.

Baddeley, A. D. (2000). The episodic buffer: A new component of working memory? *Trends in Cognitive Sciences* 4(11): 417-423.

Barbara, A. L., Freebairn, L., Tag, J., Ciesla, A. A., Iyengar, S. K., Stein, C. M., & Taylor, H. G. (2015). Adolescent outcomes of children with early speech sound disorders with and without language impairment. *American Journal of Speech Language Pathology* 24(2):150-163.

Bell, N. (1997). *Seeing stars: Symbol imagery for phonemic awareness, sight words and spelling*. Avila Beach: Gander Publishing.

Bell, N. (1986). *Visualizing and verbalizing for language comprehension and thinking*. Avila Beach: Gander Publishing.

Bull, R., & Scerif, G. (2010). Executive functioning as a predictor of children's mathematics ability: Inhibition, switching, and working memory. *Developmental Neuropsychology* 19(3):273-293.

Carlson, H., Sugden, C., Kirton, A., & Brooks, B. L. (2018). Neuroplasticity of functional connectivity in language networks in children after perinatal stroke. *Stroke* 49:ATMP103.

Carpenter, P. A., Just, M. A., & Reichle, E. D. (2000). Working memory and executive functions: Evidence from neuroimaging. *Current Opinion in Neurobiology* 10:195–199.

Cohen, L., Lehericy, S., Chochon, F., Lemer, C., Rivaud, S., & Dehaene, S. (2002). Language specific tuning of visual cortex? Functional properties of the visual word form area. *Brain* 125(5):1054-1069.

Dawson, P. & Guare, R. (2018). *Executive skills in children and adolescents: A Practical Guide to Assessment and Intervention. Third Edition*. New York: The Guilford Press.

Dehaene, S., Pegado, F., Braga, L. W., Ventura, P., Nunes Filho, G., Jobert, A., Dehaene-Lambertz, G., Kolinsky, R., Morais, J., & Cohen, L. (2010). How learning to read changes the cortical networks for vision and language. *Science* 330(6009):1359-1364.

Dehn, M. J. (2008). *Working memory and academic learning: Assessment and intervention*. New Jersey: John Wiley & Sons, Inc.

Dodd, B., & Gillon, G. (2009). Exploring the relationship between phonological awareness, speech impairment, and literacy. *Advances in Speech Language Pathology* 3(2):139-147.

Drazinski, L. A. (2011). *Executive functions training: Adolescent*. Austin: LinguiSystems, Inc.

Falik, L. H., & Feuerstein, R. S. (2015). *Changing minds and brains: The legacy of Reuven Feuerstein, higher thinking and cognition through mediated learning*. New York: Teachers College Press.

Fazio, B. B. (1996). Mathematical abilities of children with specific language impairment: A 2-year follow-up. *Journal of Speech, Language, and Hearing Research* 39(4):839-849.

Felsenfeld, S., Broen, P.A., & McGue, M. (1994). A 28-year follow-up of adults with a history of moderate phonological disorder: Educational and occupational results. *Journal of Speech and Hearing Research* 37(6):1341-1353.

Feuerstein, R., & Falik, L. H. (2010). Learning to think, thinking to learn: A comprehensive analysis of three approaches to instruction. *Journal of Cognitive Education and Psychology* 9(1):4-20.

Feuerstein, R., Feuerstein, R. S., Falik, L., & Rand, Y. (2006). *Creating and enhancing cognitive modifiability: The Feuerstein Instrumental Enrichment Program. Part 1, Theoretical and conceptual foundations. Part 2, Practical applications of the Feuerstein Instrumental Enrichment Program*. ICELP Publications.

Guarnera, M., Commodari, E., & Peluso, C. (2013). Rotation and generation of mental imagery in children with specific language impairment. *ACTA PAEDIATRICA: Nurturing The Child* 102(5):539-543.

Guarnera, M., Faraci, P., Commodari, E., & Buccheri, S. L. (2017). Mental imagery and school readiness. *Psychological Reports* 120(6):1058-1077.

Hood, M., & Conlon, E. (2004). Visual and auditory temporal processing and early reading development. *Dyslexia* 10(3):234-252.

Horgan, J. (1991). "Profile: Physicist John A. Wheeler, Questioning the 'it from bit.'" *Scientific American* 264(6):36-37. Quote attributed to Einstein by physicist John Archibald Wheeler.

James, K. H. (2009). Sensori-motor experience leads to changes in visual processing in the developing brain. *Developmental Science* 13:279–288.

Kolb, B., & Gibb, R. (2011). Brain plasticity and behaviour in the developing brain. *Journal of the Canadian Academy of Child and Adolescent Psychiatry* 20(4):265–276.

Kolker, B., & Terwiliger, P. N. (1986). Visual imagery of text and children's processing. *Reading Psychology* 7(4):267-277.

Lindamood, P. C., & Lindamood, P. D. (1998). *The Lindamood phoneme sequencing program for reading, spelling, and speech.* Austin: PRo-ED.

Mazoyer, B., Zago, L., Mellet, E., Bricogne, S., Etard, O., Houde, O., Crivello, F., Joliot, M., Petit, L., & Tzourio-Mazoyer, N. (2001). Cortical networks for working memory and executive functions sustain the conscious resting state in man. *Brain Research Bulletin* 54(3):287-298.

McCabe, D. P., Roediger, III, H. L., McDaniel, M. A., Balota, D. A., & Hambrick, D. Z. (2010). The relationship between working memory capacity and executive functioning: Evidence for a common executive attention construct. *Neuropsychology* 24(2):222-243.

McCloskey, G. (2015). *Improving executive functions.* PESI rehab seminar.

McCloskey, G., & Perkins, L. A. (2012). *Essentials of executive functions assessment.* New York: Wiley.

McCloskey, G., Perkins, L. A., & VanDivner, B. (2009). *Assessment and intervention for executive function difficulties.* New York: Routledge Press.

McNeill, B. C., Gillon, G. T., & Dodd, B. (2009). Phonological awareness and early reading development in childhood apraxia of speech (CAS). *International Journal of Language and Communication Disorders* 44(2):175-192.

Mei, L., Xue, G., Chen, C., Xue, F., Zhang, M., & Donga, Q. (2010). The "visual word form area" is involved in successful memory encoding of both words and faces. *Neuroimage* 52(1):371–378.

Miller, G. J., Lewis, B., Benchek, P., Freebairn, L., Tag, J., Budge, K., Iyengar, S. K., Voss-Hoynes, H., Gerry Taylor, H., & Stein, C. (2019). Reading outcomes for individuals with histories of suspected childhood apraxia of speech. *American Journal of Speech Language Pathology* 28(4):1432-1447.

Moon, C., Lagercrantz, H., & Kuhl, P. K. (2013). Language experienced *in utero* affects vowel perception after birth: A two-country study. *Acta Paediatrica* 102(2):156-160.

Munson, B., & Krause, M. O. P. (2017). Phonological encoding in speech sound disorder: Evidence from a cross-modal priming experiment. *International Journal of Language and Communication Disorders* 52(3):285-300.

Nathan, L., Stackhouse, J., Goulandris, N., & Snowling, M. J. (2004). The development of early literacy skills among children with speech difficulties: A test of the "critical age hypothesis." *Journal of Speech Language and Hearing Research* 47(2):377-391.

Pauls, L. J., & Archibald, L. M. D. (2016). Executive functions in children with specific language impairment: A meta-analysis. *Journal of Speech, Language, and Hearing Research* 59(5):1074-1086.

Pinker, S. (2008). "Language and consciousness Part I: Are our thoughts constrained by language? With Steven Pinker. Ph.D." *Thinking Allowed: Conversations on the Leading Edge of Knowledge and Discovery with Dr. Jeffrey Mishlove.* http://www.williamjames.com/transcripts/pinker1.htm.

Poeppel, D., Idsardi, W. J., & van Wassenhove, V. (2008). Speech perception at the interface of neurobiology and linguistics. *Philosophical Transactions of the Royal Society B* 363 (1493):1071–1086.

Rey, V., De Martino, S., Espesser, R., & Habib, M. (2002). Temporal processing and phonological impairment in dyslexia: Effect of phoneme lengthening on order judgment of two consonants. *Brain and Language* 80:576–591.

Rvachew, S., & Grawburg, M. (2006). Correlates of phonological awareness in preschoolers with speech sound disorders. *Journal of Speech, Language, and Hearing Research* 49(1):74-87.

Scarborough, H. S., Neuman, S. B., & Dickinson, D. K. (2001). *Handbook of early literacy research.* New York: Guilford Press.

Smith, L. B., & Sheya, A. (2010). Is cognition enough to explain cognitive development? *Topics in Cognitive Science* 2(4):725-735.

Smolak, E., McGregor, K., Arbisi-Kelm, T., & Eden, N. (2020). Sustained attention in developmental language disorder and its relation to working memory and language. *Journal of Speech, Language, and Hearing Research* 63(12):4096-4108.

Wagner, R. K., & Torgesen, J. K. (1987). The nature of phonological processing and its causal role in the acquisition of reading skills. *Psychological Bulletin 101*:192-212.

Watson, B. U., & Miller, T. K. (1993). Auditory perception, phonological processing, and reading ability/disability. *Journal of Speech, Language, and Hearing Research* 36(4):850-863.

Windsor, J., Kohnert, K., Loxtercamp, A. L., & Kan, P-F. (2008). Performance on nonlinguistic visual tasks by children with language impairment. *Applied Psycholinguistics* 29(2):237-268.

Made in the USA
Monee, IL
23 April 2021

66645653R00069